The Third Book of

COTSWOLD RAMBLES

21 Short Walks in the Finest Part of the Cotswolds

Harry Hargreaves

Note: All these rambles are different from those in *Cotswold Rambles* Books I & II

Published by
Thornhill Press
24 Moorend Road
Cheltenham

THORNHILL PRESS
Cheltenham
MCMLXXXVIII

ISBN 0 946328 20 X

Cover photograph: ULEYBURY

Typeset by Wessex Typesetters
(Division of The Eastern Press Ltd)
Frome, Somerset
and Printed by
The Devonshire Press Ltd
Torquay, Devon

Authors' Note

As we have wandered in the Cotswolds for many months we decided that the First and Second Book of Cotswold Rambles could be followed by a Third Book which, because of our joint experience, would be entirely new and would perhaps be even more interesting than the others. Some of the walks are in areas which we have discovered recently and have the added interest of such remoteness that they will make many ramblers aware of country which would otherwise be missed.

We appreciate the debt we owe to those associations and authorities which have contributed to the keeping open and protection of the countryside.

We also wish to express our thanks to the many farmers and landowners who have been helpful in removing obstructions and have co-operated in the clearance and the waymarking of footpaths.

Richard Burlingham
Fred Evans
Harry Hargreaves
Fred Heathfield
David Hughes
Max Lovatt
Tony Lyon
Herbert Watts

The Third Book of Cotswold Rambles

Introduction

This book contains approximately 110 miles of rambling. The shortest ramble is 3 miles and the longest 9 miles. Although they are described as short walks, 'short' should not be thought of as 'easy'. They are not gentle strolls but require care and concentration. Allow more than 1 hour for each 2 miles of walking.

The rambles are in that part of the Cotswolds between Chipping Campden in the north and Wotton-under-Edge in the south, an area of infinite variety and charm.

The narrative of each ramble is so detailed that it should not be necessary to use a map. At the beginning of each ramble the appropriate Ordnance Survey Map number is stated. The printed map at the beginning of each ramble gives an outline of the ramble and can be followed with each narrative. These maps have all been done by Mr. Fred Heathfield and the authors are appreciative of the skill with which they have been produced. If the rambler departs from the narrative because of some interest or through lack of attention to the narrative these maps should help to get back to the right way.

It is stating the obvious to say; make sure you get to the right starting point, otherwise everything is wrong.

At the beginning of each ramble a place which is the starting point or from which the starting point will be approached is named and on the map on the back cover that place will have the number of the ramble related to it.

Each ramble starts and finishes at the same place.

Whilst every endeavour has been made to ensure that each ramble follows throughout its length the existing Rights of Way and care has been taken to ensure the accuracy of all information in the book, the Authors and Publisher cannot accept any liability for the accuracy of the information given or for its interpretation by readers.

THE COUNTRY CODE

Please remember as you walk throughout the countryside to respect the privacy and livelihood of those who live in the country. The Country Code asks you to:

1. Guard against all risk of fire.
2. Fasten all gates
3. Keep dogs under proper control.
4. Keep to paths across farmland.
5. Avoid damaging fences, hedges and walls.
6. Leave no litter.
7. Safeguard water supplies.
8. Protect wild life, plants and trees.
9. Go carefully on country roads.
10. Respect the life of the countryside.

Contents

RAMBLE 1

Ebrington–Broad Campden

Distance: $6\frac{1}{2}$ miles. Map OS 151 in the 1:50000 series and SP 03/13 in the 1:25000 Pathfinder series.
Starting point: Grid reference 184399 – the village of Ebrington.

To get to Ebrington from Chipping Campden go past the church and go along B4035 for 2 miles.

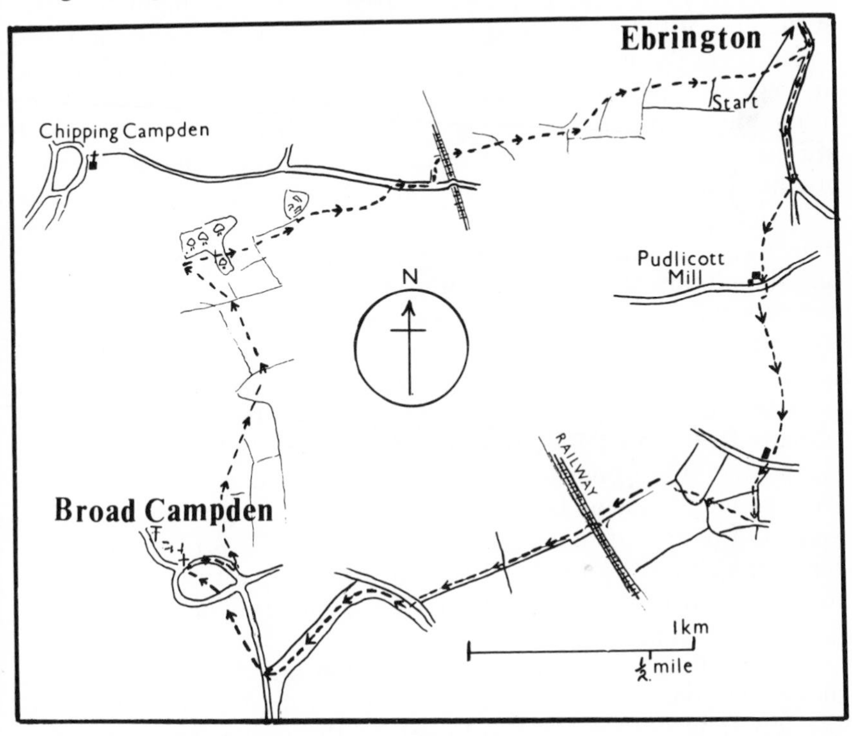

From the Three Oaks Inn walk south along May Lane. In $\frac{1}{2}$ mile, when the road goes to the left, take a footpath on the right. (Avoid the footpath on the right which precedes this at some farm buildings.)

Keep near to a hedge on the left along a wide farm track. In 100 yards where the farm track goes to the right leave it to go into the green track on the left and continue alongside a stream and hedge and a series of ponds. Keep these ponds on the left and continue to a farm track. Turn left and pass to the left of Pudlicott Mill to the road. Cross the road and go over the stile opposite. Turn right and go ahead with the brook on the right. At the end of the second field cross the farm track and continue ahead with the brook still on the right to the road. Turn right over the road bridge and immediately take the signposted footpath on the left.

Walk with the brook on the left. At the end of the field where there is a farm bridge on the left (DO NOT CROSS) turn right and walk across the field to the woodland ahead. At the woodland, search for a substantial wide farm bridge, which cross. (If there are growing crops, instead of walking across the field, it might be better at the end of the above field to turn right and walk along the fence which is on the left to the corner of the field. Here turn right and in 150 yards the above bridge is arrived at.) Having crossed the bridge turn immediately right and follow the brook and hedge which are on the right to the corner of the field. Turn left and in 40 yards go through the wicket gate on the right into the adjoining field. Turn left and follow the hedge which is on the left to the railway line. Cross the railway line (take care, there are frequent trains) and then follow the hedge which is on the left to the road.

Cross the road, enter the wood and in a few yards follow the footpath as it goes to the right. Go ahead, cross a farm track and go straight ahead as indicated by a waymark. When the path comes near to the road locate a signposted path on the right (sometimes obscured). Follow this to the road. Cross the road and go over the signposted stile opposite. Descend to the right and go through a wide gap in the facing hedge. Continue the descent to a waymarked stile. Go over and down some steps and pass over another way-marked stile to the road. Cross into the footpath opposite which leads to St. Michael's Church, Broad Campden. (The Bakers Arms is on the main road to the left.)

Turn right down the road signposted 'Unsuitable for Motors'. Go along this road for 200 yards and then just past a large house on the left (and before some cottages on the right) turn left where there is a stone public path notice. Go through a gate marked Holly Bush and continue to a second gate waymarked. Continue to another waymarked gate. Pass through and go straight ahead as indicated by one of two waymarks. In about 100 yards go over the waymarked stile on the right.

Go ahead with a fence on the left. In about 100 yards, and about 15 yards before the boundary of the field, pass over the fence on the left and cross a waymarked stile and footbridge and turn right.

Follow the hedge and stream which are on the right to where this stream makes a junction with a water course at the end of the field. About 25 yards to the left pass through a gap over an earth bridge into the next field. The way is straight across the field, about equidistant from the hedge on each side, to a gap in the facing fence which pass through into the next field. Ascend this field walking parallel to the hedge on the left but about 50 yards from it, to a stile in the facing hedge.

Cross the stile and Chipping Campden Church can be seen north west. Go diagonally left passing between two large trees in the middle of the field to the corner of the field. There is a stile in this corner; do *NOT* cross but turn sharp right along the boundary of the same field with a woodland on the left. At a point where the woodland juts out to the right go into the wood over a stile. Pass through this wood and on coming out of it over a stile go ahead in the same direction across the field and pass into the next field and go ahead with the boundary hedge immediately on the left. Still continue ahead as the River Cam becomes obvious on the left. At the end of this field pass into the next field over a stile. Go ahead roughly in the same direction (east) across this open field to the road.

Turn right. In about 200 yards, before the road passes over the railway, turn left down a signposted drive. Go to the left of some buildings and pass over a waymarked stile. Turn right over the railway lines (take care, frequent trains) and cross the waymarked stile opposite. Go in the direction indicated by the waymark to arrive at a facing hedge at a footbridge over a brook.

Pass over the footbridge and then go diagonally right and pass to the left of two large trees in the middle of the field to a waymarked stile. Cross the small footbridge and then go in the direction of a gap between two lines of poplars and pass through a gate. Make for the left hand end of the right line of poplars to a waymarked stile.

Over the stile go ahead along the definite track which leads back to Ebrington.

RAMBLE 2
Dover's Hill, Chipping Campden, Broad Campden

A walk which starts from a National Trust Area and goes through two typical Cotswold villages.
Distance: 5 miles. Map OS 151 in the 1:50000 series and SP 03/13 in the 1:25000 Pathfinder series.
Starting point: Grid reference 137396. Dover's Hill near Chipping Campden.

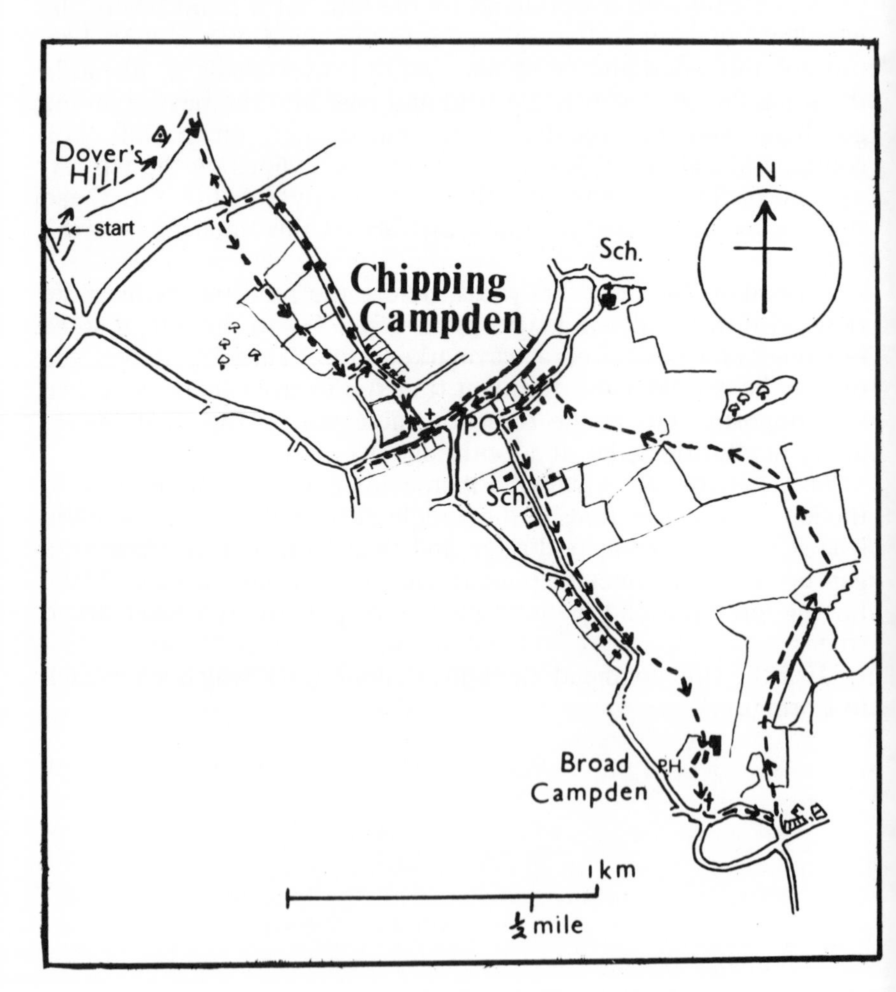

To get to Dover's Hill from Chipping Campden go up Dyers Lane. Go over the cross roads and in 200 yards turn right into the Dovers Hill car park.

In the beginning of the 17th century Dover's Hill was the site of some vigorous and roisterous Games. These on occasions lead to some debauchery. They were suppressed during the Puritan Period resurrected again later and passed through other vicissitudes which lead to them being abolished. The site passed to the National Trust in 1929.

Beginning of the walk

Go through the wicket gate and follow the hedge on the right. In about 400 yards there is a stone pillar with the emblem of the National Trust. Seventy yards past this go over the stile on the right with the Cotswold Way sign; a yellow arrow and a white dot. Follow the hedge which is on the left to the road.

Turn right for 10 yards and then turn left into a field with a footpath signpost. Follow the direction indicated by the signpost and pick up and follow the stiles and yellow waymarks to a farm. Pass to the right of the farm buildings to a facing hedge with a waymark. Go through, turn left and follow footpath waymarks. On coming to the road turn left and then look for a footpath signpost 30 yards on the right. Follow the footpath through to the road; turn right to the main street of Chipping Campden.

Turn left; at the Post Office on the right go through an archway and through the yard of the Noel Arms Inn.

On coming out of the Noel Arms Inn courtyard go straight ahead up George Lane. George Lane narrows at the intersection with Pear Tree Close. Keep straight ahead with school playing fields on the right. Just before coming to the road pass into a footpath on the left. Go ahead across a farm road and continue with a hedge on the right which runs parallel to the road. At the point where the road swings to the right away from the path continue ahead up the definite ascending path, a green track. In about 170 yards there are two waymarked tracks, take the one to the right and continue with an overgrown wall on the left to a wicket gate. Pass through and go ahead with a house on the left. Just past this house leave the drive and go to the left as indicated by a footpath signpost. Pass through a wicket gate and go along a narrow path on emerging from which there is a Quaker Meeting House. Turn right down the metalled lane to St. Michael's Church, Broad Campden (the Bakers Arms Inn is to the right).

Turn left down the road signposted 'unsuitable for motorists'. Go along this road for 200 yards and then just past a large house on the left (and before some cottages ahead on the right) turn left where there is a stone public path notice. Go through a gate marked 'Holly Bush'. Go ahead to pass through a waymarked gate and continue to another gate. There are two waymarks here; take the one straight ahead. In about 100 yards go over the waymarked stile on the right. Go ahead with a fence close on the right. Fifteen yards before a facing fence descend to the left, cross a waymarked stile and footbridge and turn right.

Follow the hedge and stream which are on the right to where the stream makes a junction with a water course. About 25 yards to the left pass through a gap over an earth bridge into the next field. The way is straight across the field (20°E of N) about equidistant from the hedge on each side to a gap in the facing hedge which pass through into the next field. Ascend the field, walking parallel to the hedge on the left but about 50 yards from it to a stile in the facing hedge.

Cross the stile and Chipping Campden church can be seen north west. Go diagonally left to the corner of the field and pass over a stile. Go straight across to a line of trees bordering the River Cam. Turn left and continue ahead close to these trees. Go past an isolated stone arch (see photograph) to a wicket gate on the right. Go through and cross a footbridge over a stream. Go on to a rubble road. Turn right. On coming to the road (Calf Lane) turn left. Continue along to where Calf Lane merges into George Lane. Turn right to pass through the yard of the Noel Arms Inn on to the main road. Turn left. At the Catholic Church turn right. Follow the Cotswold Way signs uphill to the lane. Turn left and in 100 yards take the signposted Cotswold Way footpath on the right. Follow the hedge which is on the right for about 400 yards and pass over a stile onto Dover's Hill. Turn left to the car park which is the end and beginning of the walk.

(Walk 2)

Looking towards St. James church, Chipping Camden

RAMBLE 3
Ebrington–Foxcote–Ilmington

Distance: 9 miles. Map OS 151 in the 1:50000 series and SP 04/14 and SP 24/34 in the 1:25000 Pathfinder series.
Starting point: Grid reference 185400: the village of Ebrington.

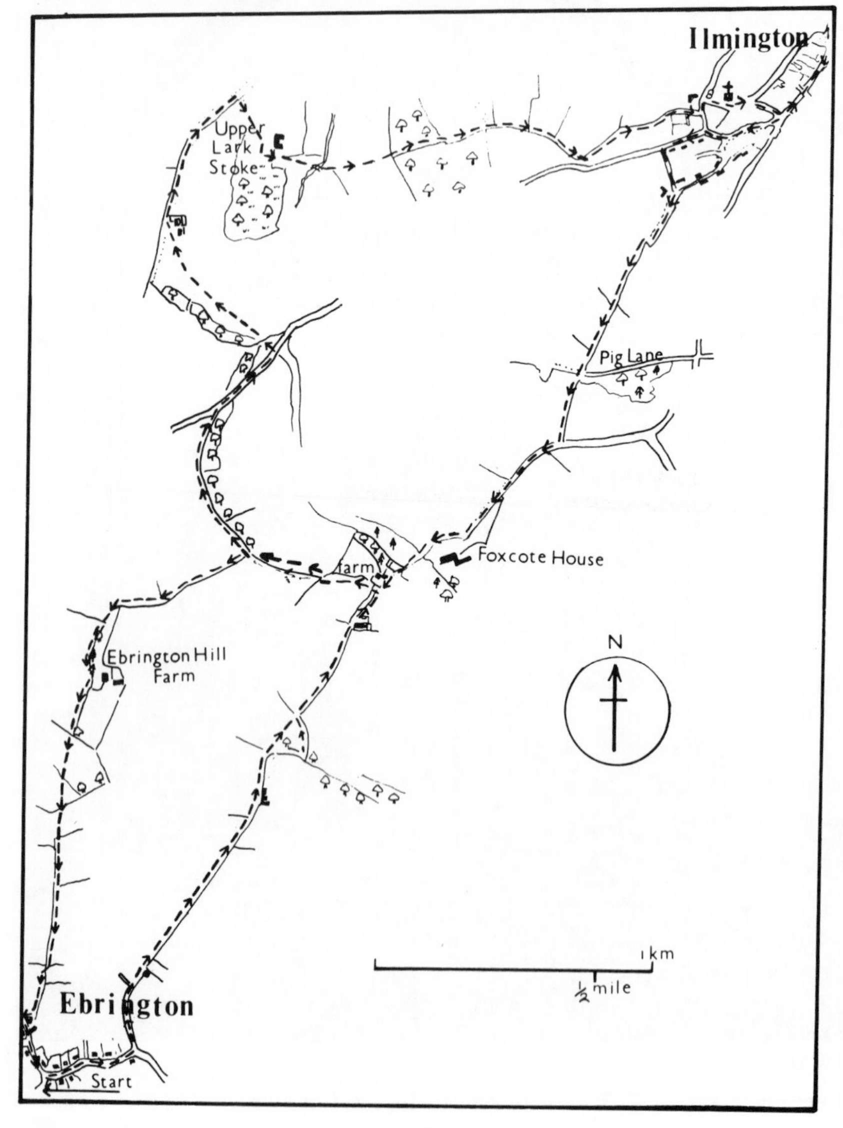

To get to Ebrington from Chipping Campden, go past the church and continue along B4035 for 2 miles.

From the Three Oaks Inn and with the War Memorial at your back take the signposted Shipston road, B4035, and walk downhill past the telephone kiosk. Take the first road left – by a letter box – marked 'No through road'. It continues as a track in a NE direction. Pass three large barns and continue, with the hedge on the right, downhill. At the bottom of the bank leave the path where it swings right and cross the stream (county boundary).

Ascend the hill in front bearing slightly right towards the left of three trees on the skyline. (If there are growing crops it is easier to use the track to the right round the headland.) At the tree go through a gate and immediately right to resume the NE direction of the walk, alongside a wire fence on the right. Pass through a double metal gate and keeping the farm buildings on the right, go on for 150 yards to Foxcote Farm. A few yards before the farm go left along a fence and through a metal gate into a field.

Go half right ascending field towards the facing hedge to reach a stile 70 yards to the left of power lines. Cross, and proceed ahead to follow the headland up the slope of the field, with the hedge on the left, to a copse. Continue along the left of it for 500 yards to a metalled road. Turn right and in 400 yards go left through a gate which is directly opposite a drive marked 'To Foxcote House'. Cross the short distance to the facing gate. Pass through and cross the next field keeping a copse about 80 yards on the left. Aim towards the farm buildings of Stoke Hill Barn.

At the metalled track, 50 yards past the barn, turn right and follow the hedge on the left downhill for 300 yards to its end. Continue downhill for a further 200 yards passing three large trees on the right. Just past the last tree, where the hedge ends, turn right and proceed in a SE direction across cultivated land. Aim at the left hand side of the two aerial masts on the skyline. At the field boundary cross a ditch to enter a broad ride into a new plantation. Proceed ahead and in 70 yards, at a waymarked post, turn left to descend to, and go through, a small iron gate. (Upper Larkstoke Farm is about 100 yards on the left.) Continue in the same direction downhill across a field and cross the stream by an earthen bridge.

Go through a small wooden gate and veer left. In 50 yards, at the hedge, cross the stream by a waymarked stile, bridge and stile. Walk up the facing field, as the waymark directs over the highest visible point and down in the same direction to a waymarked gate and stile. Cross the next field with a wooden fence on the right and go through the facing iron gate into a track with a wooden fence on each side. Pass through two more gates and bear right when you join a track coming from a large barn some distance on the left. Continue ahead and pass through another gate. At a gate and waymarked stile on the left of track, rather than using the main road ahead, bear left over the stile and walk, with the hedge on the left, across pasture. Aim for Ilmington church tower.

At this point of the walk, overlooking Ilmington, the views are superb. Pass down a dark lane between some holly bushes and turn left at the main road. In 40 yards take a footpath on the right to the church and pass its main door. Note the sundial on the tower. Follow the path to the left round the church and continue ahead to the main road. At the main road turn left and walk 200 yards to the Red Lion, Ilmington, where good beer and food can be obtained from the welcoming Landlord.

On leaving the Red Lion inn go to the right, going right at the first main fork past a memorial to the first providers of pure water to the village. Go up the road signposted Ebrington and Campden for 300 yards and look on the left for a low stone stile and waymark. Cross and descend, then rise between gardens, turning right at the road. It becomes a green track. Just before a facing farm gate is a waymark on the right. Go down slope and cross the stile and the second facing stile. Turn sharp left with wire fence on the left and walk up three fields to Pig Lane. Cross lane and walk down field with hedge on the left. At road turn right, pass Foxcote House and at Foxcote Farm go the same way to the copse as that done earlier in the walk. Just before the start of the copse, turn sharp left along the field boundary hedge, with the hedge on the left, direction SW. Follow it when it turns sharp left to a wood, and turn sharp right for 40 yards alongside the fence bordering the wood to a stile on the left. Cross stile and follow the waymarked posts ahead, on the outside of wood. Continue ahead along the field headland with a wire fence on the left, and walk through next field in same direction.

At a gap in the facing hedge cross next field bearing slightly left – due S – to another gap in the facing hedge, about 50 yards to the right of a clump of trees. Cross the next field using Ebrington Church as a marker, cross a stile in the hedge and down the next field to pass through a wicket gate. Continue in the same direction over a stile and footbridge in the corner of the field. Keeping the hedge on the right reach the corner of the field and cross the stile and turn left.

Walk with the iron fence on the left, go over a stile and through a farm gate and thence to road. Go left through Ebrington to return to The Three Oaks Inn.

RAMBLE 4

Broadway–Coneygree Lane–Kite's Nest–Broadway Road–Middle Hill

A varied walk with splendid views.
Distance: 7 miles. Map OS 150 in 1:50000 series and Pathfinder Series Sheet SP 03/13 – Broadway & Chipping Campden 1:25000
Starting point: Grid reference 102376: car park on the A46 Willersey Road, Broadway.

Turn left out of car park and walk to A44 (main Oxford Road). Turn left; in about 200 yards and 40 yards past Milestone Hotel take a public footpath on the right signposted Broadway Tower.

Follow the Cotswold Way signs (yellow arrow and white spot) to the National Trust sign Clump Farm. Go through the passage ahead in the corner of the field and through the gate on the right with the Cotswold Way sign. In 40 yards leave the Cotswold Way and take the sunken track on the right. This leads to a gate at the boundary of the field. Pass through and follow the left hand wall boundary of the field which consists of some intermittent trees and a ruined wall. This becomes a definite track which descends to a line of trees running down to the right. Descend to the left of these trees to a rough lane. This is Coneygree Lane. Turn right down this lane to the Broadway–Snowshill road opposite the old Broadway Church.

About the 14th century Coneygree Lane was the main road which came to the middle of the then village of Broadway, at the church. Later the main road came down Fish Hill and the centre of the village moved to what is now the main A44 road.

Turn left and in about $\frac{1}{2}$ mile turn up a cart track to Kite's Nest Farm.

This farm is interesting because it is run on completely organic principles.

At the end of the avenue of poplars continue ahead through the farm buildings. Immediately past the last building – an imposing farmhouse on the right – turn right and descend to and cross the stream and follow the track round to the left.

Continue along and up this track and in less than $\frac{1}{4}$ mile Broadway Wood cottages are reached. These have been converted into holiday accommodation. Immediately before these cottages there are two

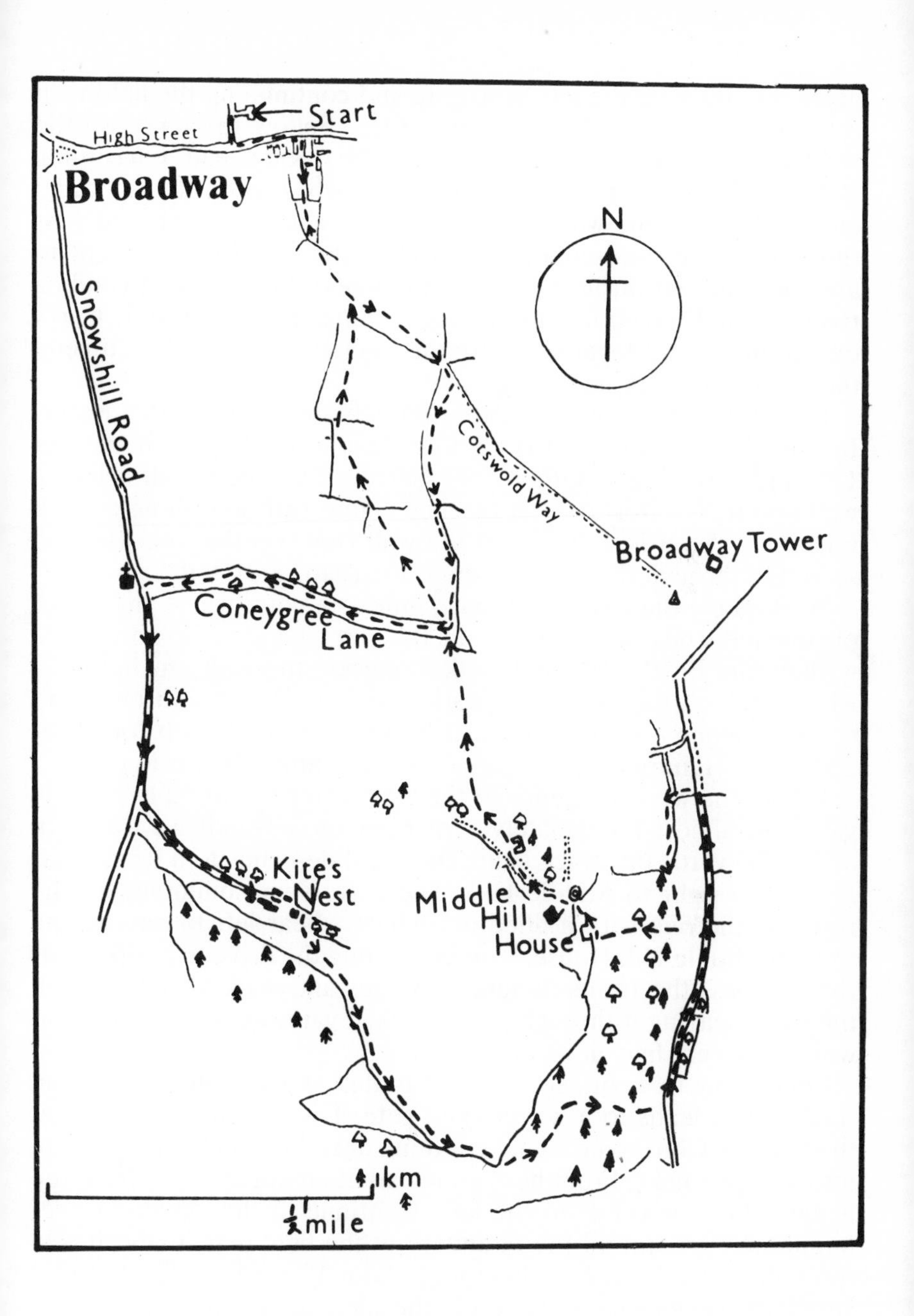
Start
High Street
Broadway
N
Snowshill Road
Cotswold Way
Broadway Tower
Coneygree
Lane
Kite's
Nest
Middle
Hill
House
1km
½mile

gates. Go through the left hand gate and continue up the field with a fence on the right. Go through a gate. Follow the fence on the right as it veers left and ascend towards the wood ahead. On coming to the end of the fence, follow the wood which is on the right and enclosed by a stone wall. Continue on for about 150 yards to pass through a gate. Still continue to follow the wood on the right to another gate: go through to enter the wood. Follow the ascending track. At a T junction with a very definite track, turn left. Carry on and in about 200 yards, where the track bends to the left, ascend the woodland track on the right.

In about 60 yards cross a definite track and continue the ascent. In a further 150 yards cross another definite track, and in another 120 yards cross yet another one. Carry on ascending till a facing wall about 30 yards away is reached. Here turn left along a track for about 25 yards till a gap in the wall (now on the right) will be seen. Go through this gap and on to the road. Turn left.

Walk along the road for about ¾ mile to a point where the wood on the left ends and a wood on the right begins. Go through a wicket gate on the left and walk alongside the wall on the left – which encloses the wood – to another wicket gate. Pass through and continue along a definite track with the wood on the left for about 250 yards. (Ignore a barred gate on the left after 100 yards.)

Where the wood descends to the right enter the wood by an iron gate and almost immediately turn right on a woodland track. In about 200 yards this track bears right and descends to a farm road. Here turn right to Middle Hill. There are some buildings on the right: at the one with a filled-in archway, bear left to pass to the right of Middle Hill House. Continue along the drive to a fork: bear right to pass the fronts of some cottages and walk ahead through the wood leaving it through a waymarked gateway. Carry on ahead with some very fine views on the left.

On coming to a cottage, veer left to descend and pick up a green track which leads to a waymarked gate. Pass through to arrive at the head of Coneygree Lane: continue ahead through another gate into an open field. From here go ahead at an angle of 45° from the hedge which descends to the left. Continue in this direction over hummocky ground till the boundary of the field is seen ahead. Go through a gate (a stile is alongside) about 15 yards on the left of a very large beech tree. Carry on in the same direction passing to the left of a large tree and gradually descend to the boundary hedge on the left. Where this hedge turns left and then, at a gate turns right, follow parallel to the hedge to arrive at a facing boundary hedge with a stile. Cross this stile and the little water course and in 40 yards turn left down a definite track. (This is the track which leads up to National Trust sign Crump Farm at the beginning of the walk.) Follow the Cotswold signs back into Broadway and then go on to the car park from where the walk started.

(Walk 4)

Near Middle Hill

RAMBLE 5

A walk from Blockley with some good views

Distance: 3 miles. Map OS 151 in the 1:50000 series. Map SP 03/13 in the Pathfinder 1:25000 series.
Starting point: Grid reference 164349: village of Blockley.

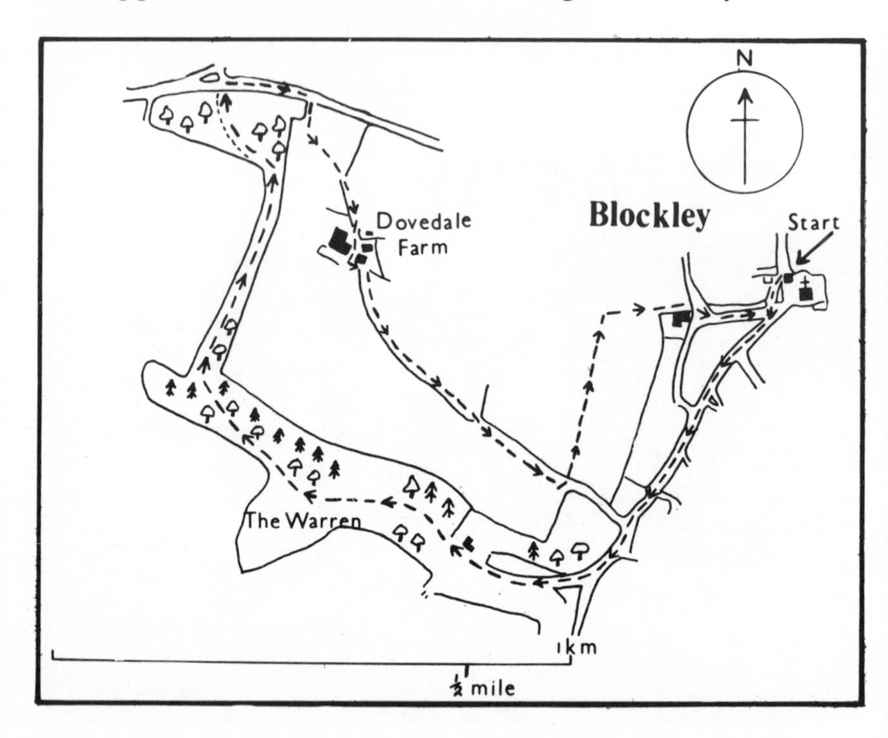

Go along the main street with the Crown Hotel on the right, and immediately after Vine Cottage, turn right at a post box up the cart-track marked 'Public Footpath'. The first cottage here has an interesting memorial to an old trout that died a century ago. In about 200 yards fork right and continue through the wood for a mile to the road.

Turn right on the road and, in about 150 yards, take the concreted drive on the right marked Dovedale Farm. Pass through the farm and, immediately after the last building, turn left and then in 30 yards right to follow the remains of a former hedge, keeping it on the right. In about 300 yards turn right into the adjoining field at a point where the remains of a stone wall and a gatepost are still visible.

Turn left to follow the ditch and remains of the wall and hedge towards the cottage at the bottom end of the field.

Immediately before the cottage, and without passing through the gate, turn left at right angles to the path and in the direction shown by the footpath sign across the open field. A wall is shown across this field on the map but it has recently been removed. In 300 yards, at a point where the church re-appears behind the cottage on the right, turn at a right angle towards it and descend to the stile at the corner of the cottage, keeping the buildings on the right. Cross the stile into Bell Bank and go down the narrow lane into Blockley.

RAMBLE 6
Blockley

A walk with some excellent views.
Distance: **3½ miles. Maps OS 151 in the 1:50000 series and SP 03/13** in the Pathfinder 1:25000 series.
Starting point: Grid reference 164349: village of Blockley.

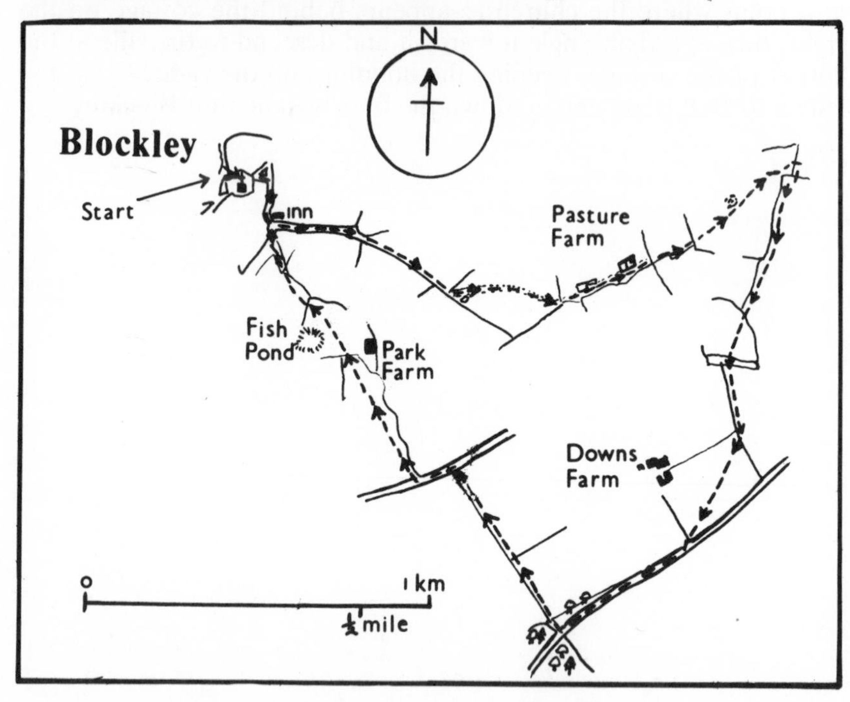

From the British Legion club go into the churchyard and walk along the path with the church on the right down to the road. Turn right and just beyond the Lower Brook Hotel take the first turn left, signposted to Pasture Farm. At the beginning the road is of tarmac but soon turns into a pebbled track. At a new barn bear left: there are now excellent views to the left.

Pass Pasture Farm to arrive immediately at two gates, one on the right being set back at an angle. Go through the left hand waymarked gate, straight ahead and up a short sunken track leading to another waymarked gate which pass through into a large field. Here turn 45 degrees to the left and strike across the field, aiming for the right hand side of a small patch of scrub which marks the site of a demolished building. Continue in the same direction towards a waymarked stile which should now be visible in the distant wire fence about 50 yards from where it joins the line of trees.

Cross the stile and turn right to follow the line of a wire fence. Cross waymarked stile and pass through a waymarked gate keeping close to the fence, uphill to a gap by some small trees. At the top of the rise and close to the trees is a waymark. Cross the top field to a waymarked gate in the middle of the wall and through this into a larger field with a paddock in the right hand near corner.

Ignore the waymarked gates on the right and continue in the same southerly direction keeping the wall on the right hand side. Follow the wall to a waymarked ladder-stile. Cross; walk diagonally as indicated, across this field to the point where the drive to Downs Farm meets the road. Go through waymarked gate to road.

Turn right along the road and in ½ mile, at a point opposite the nearest corner of Park Plantation, turn right into a broad signposted track leading to two gates. The right hand gate is waymarked. Pass through and keep the hedge and wall on the left through two fields.

A small waymarked gate leads into a track, walled on both sides. Turn left and pass immediately through another waymarked gate. In 100 yards a stile on the right is well marked and shows the way down to Blockley. Keep about 50 yards from the right hand fence then aim for bottom corner of the field. Cross waymarked stile and pass to the right of the fish pond to a waymarked gate by a stream. Go through and continue ahead to cross another waymarked gate/stile to road.

At the road turn right into Blockley.

Domesday Book recorded 12 mill wheels on Blockley Brook (500 people). It also had: 6 silk mills, an iron foundry, piano, soap and collar factories.

It was a summer residence of Bishops of Worcester and was one of the first places to be lit by electricity.

(Walk 6)

Above Blockley

RAMBLE 7
Bourton-on-the-Hill, Sezincote

Distance: 3 miles. Map OS 151 in the 1:50000 series; SP 03/13 in Pathfinder 1:25000 series.
Starting point: Grid reference 175324: Bourton-on-the-Hill.

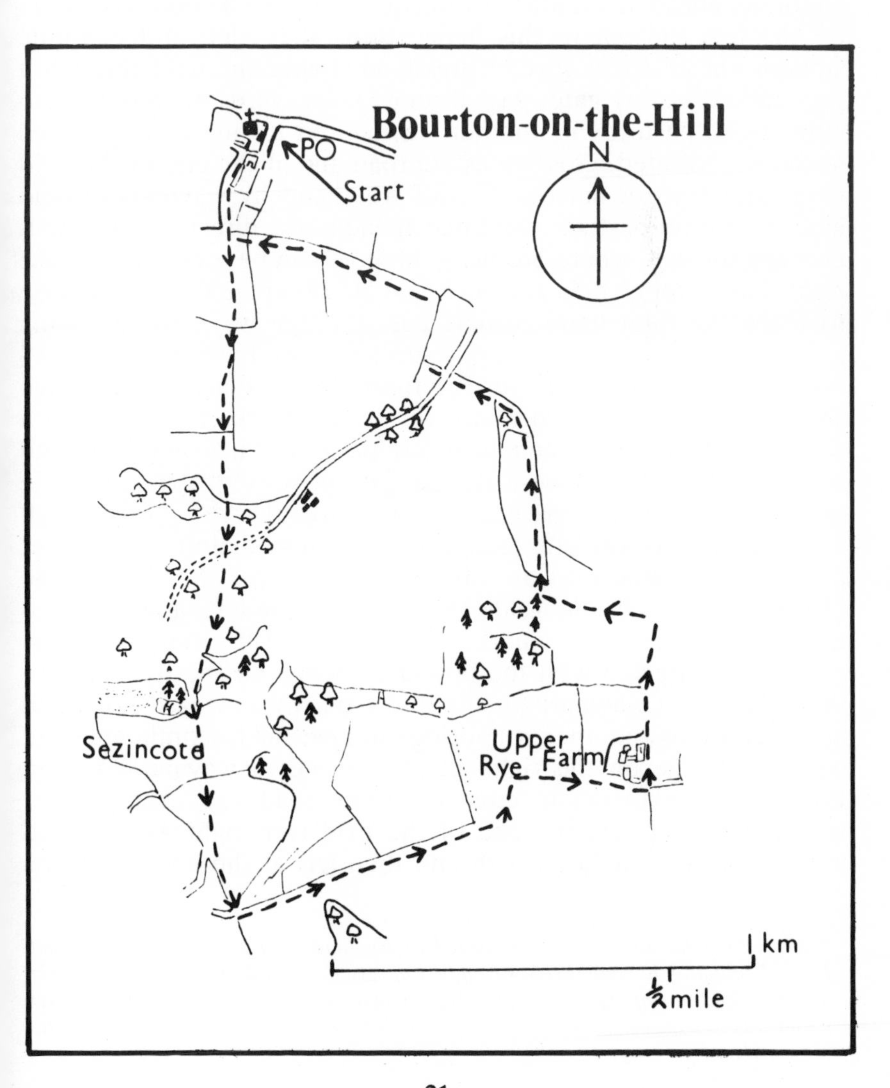

Going in the direction of Moreton-in-Marsh on A44 take the first turn right past Bourton-on-the-Hill church. In 100 yards at the telephone kiosk turn right for 50 yards and take the path on the left signposted Sezincote and Longborough. This is the start of the walk.

Proceed down the lane and in a short distance pass through field gate into pasture. Follow the definite track straight ahead to pass through another field gate into pasture and cross this field to enter a third field of meadowland via a waymarked field gate. The path continues ahead in a southerly direction alongside a boundary hedge on the left and where this hedge turns sharp left still continue straight ahead across further grassland. Leave the field through a waymarked kissing gate, pass through a few yards of woodland to enter more pasture via another waymarked kissing gate. Proceed ahead as indicated, cross an estate road and at the end of the field enter and leave a narrow strip of woodland by waymarked field gates to further pasture. Continue ahead in the direction indicated, crossing the field where Sezincote Manor* can be seen away on the right. Pass through field gate into next field keeping the same course to reach the right hand corner. Pass through waymarked kissing gate on to an estate road. Turn sharp left down the gated road for $\frac{1}{2}$ mile and where the road turns left to Upper Rye Farm continue straight on for a short distance on a farm track. Pass through a waymarked field gate and turn left past the farm buildings and continue ahead down the metalled farm drive. Cross over a cattle grid and at the end of the field, at another cattle grid, pass through a waymarked wicket gate alongside, then immediately go left over a waymarked stile into an adjacent field. Cross the field in the direction indicated, alongside the hedge on the left, and pass into the next field over a waymarked stile-bridge. Turn sharp right and proceed as directed with the boundary hedge on the right. Leave the field over a waymarked stile into a narrow enclosed track and at the end cross another stile-bridge to next field. Continue ahead with the hedge on the right and leave over a waymarked stile. Follow the waymarks to cross an estate road and over another waymarked stile. At the end of the field turn right as indicated along a narrow enclosed path and then left at the end. With the

** When Sir Charles Cockerell returned to England after serving with the East India Company he had been strongly impressed by Indian Architecture. He therefore had this manor built in the Indian style in 1805. The Prince Regent saw it and was so captivated that in 1812 he rebuilt his new pavilion in Brighton in the same style.*

boundary hedge on the right follow the waymarks ahead over three fields. Fifty yards from the field gate into the next field turn right through a metal field gate to join the path taken at beginning of walk. Continue ahead for 200 yards to reach the start.

(Walk 7)

Looking to Bourton-on-the-Hill

RAMBLE 8

Dumbleton and Alderton

A walk with magnificent views.
Distance: 6 miles. Map OS 150 in the 1:50000 series and SP 03/13 in the 1:25000 Pathfinder series.
Starting point: Grid reference 016359: Dumbleton.

Go up Dairy Lane and after the last house on the right go through a kissing gate into the grounds of Dumbleton Hall. Follow the fence on the right for about 50 yards to a stile in the fence: cross and walk diagonally left to arrive at a facing fence and waymarked stile: go over and ascend the field towards the right hand of two large conifers. Continue ahead to the wood and enter it by a waymarked stile. Walk along the definite path, over another waymarked stile and through a gate. Here turn left and follow the wood which is on the left with fine views into the valley on the right. A waymarked field gate is then reached which gives entrance to a track with wood on the left and hedge on the right.

Just beyond a gate on the right and at a point where the track takes a strong left turn go over a waymarked stile on the right. Turn left to walk parallel with the wood on the left to arrive at facing fence/hedge some 25 yards from the left hand corner of the field and pass over a waymarked stile and footbridge. Carry on across field towards Didcot Farm. Go through farm gate to the right of a large tree and continue to the farm making for the left hand end of the farm buildings. At the corner of the field turn sharp left and ascend the field following the hedge on the right. This is now the Wychavon Way.

At the top of the field go through a gate and immediately turn right into a wood and along a definite ascending track. At a cross track continue ahead, past Wychavon Way sign (*W*) on a post, and up a steep slope. Continue ahead on the definite track to the top of the ascent and look out for another *W* way sign on a post on the left of the track. Here turn left and follow a path well signposted with a hedge/fence on the left. On coming to a farm road turn right and in about 40 yards leave the *W* way at the junction of a number of tracks and turn right. In a few yards descend the middle of three tracks (signposted Alderton).

Where the track turns left, leave the wood and go through a gate on the right. Follow the hedge on a distinct path gradually downhill

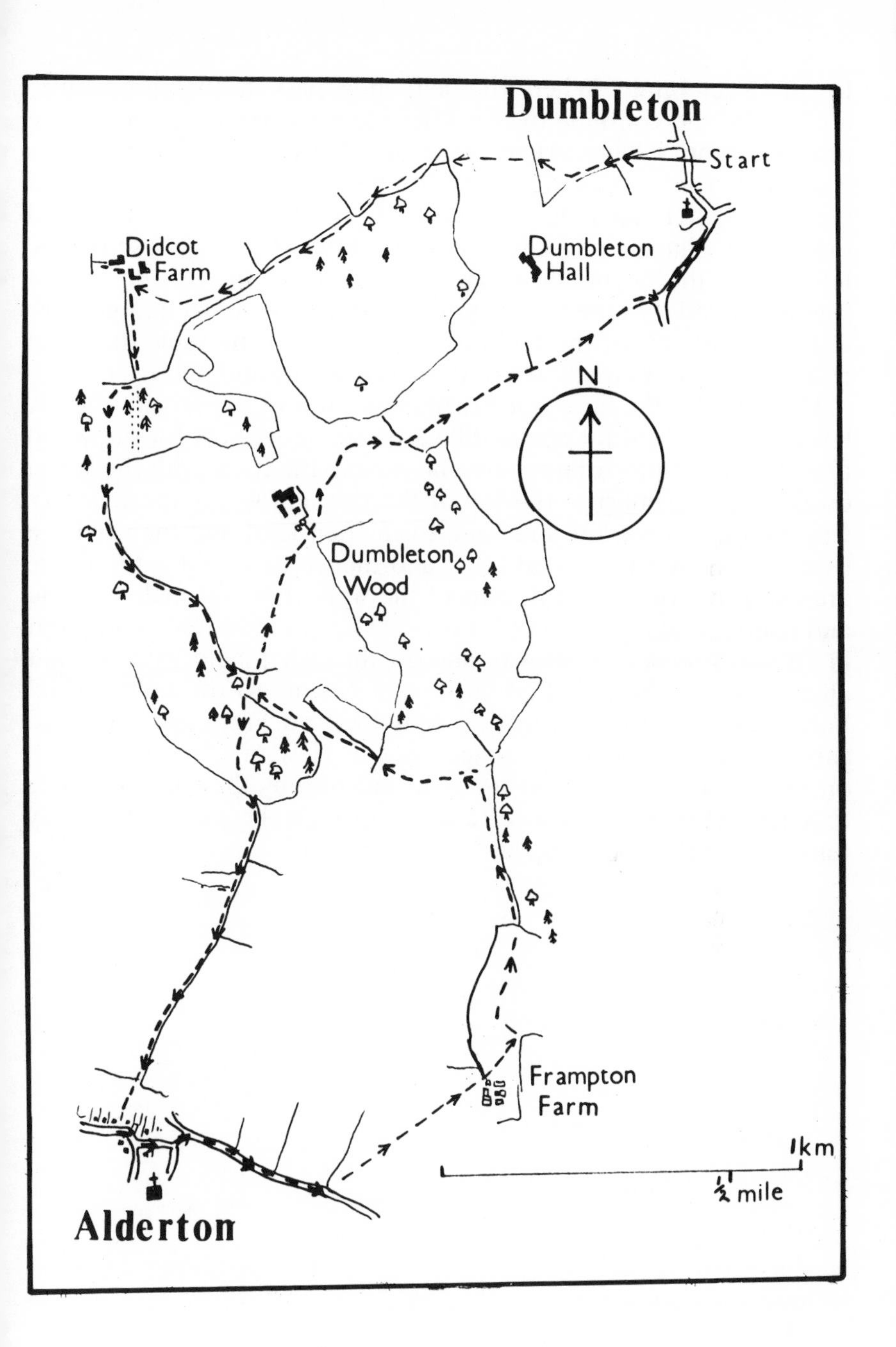
Dumbleton
Start
Didcot
Farm
Dumbleton
Hall
N
Dumbleton
Wood
Frampton
Farm
1km
½ mile
Alderton

for just over ½ mile. Where the field ends, pass through a gate into a paddock and continue over a stile into a narrow lane and thence into Alderton Village. At the road turn left (the Gardeners' Arms is about 30 yards on the right) and in a few yards at the road junction bear left to a T junction: here turn left and follow the road round out of the village along Dibden Lane. After the last house on the left and at the beginning of the third field on the left go over a signposted stile. Make for Frampton Farm seen ahead and go over a stile on the left of the buildings. Continue in the same direction to arrive at a farm track where there is a signposted pillar.

Here, where the farm track turns right, follow the *W* way slightly left across the field for about 100 yards before making for the wood ahead. Go through a farm gate and ascend the track with the wood on the right. Almost at the top of the rise and where there is a *W* way signpost, turn left and walk over open land and then, with a wood on the left to a good track and thence to a field gate. There are extensive views on this part of the walk. Pass through the gate and continue to a junction of tracks. Take the indicated *W* way but in 50 yards leave the *W* way and go through a field gate straight ahead. Follow the metalled farm road passing to the right of Hill Farm. Descend to a T junction near Leyfield Farm, turn left and carry on into Dumbleton village. A fine view of Dumbleton Hall on the left will be seen. At the road junction by the entrance gates to Dumbleton Hall, turn left, walk through the village to Dairy Lane and to the beginning and end of the walk.

RAMBLE 9

Charlton Abbots, Wontley Farm, Belas Knap, Waterhatch, Charlton Abbots

Distance: 6½ miles. Map OS 163 Cheltenham and Cirencester in the 1:50000 series, sheet SP 02/12 Stow-on-the-Wold in the Pathfinder 1:25000 series.
Starting point: Grid reference 032237: Crossroads about 700 yards south of Charlton Abbots.
There is limited parking for cars on nearby verges.

To get to the starting point from Winchcombe continue towards Cheltenham and just past the hospital take the road on the left signposted Brockhampton. Go along the road for about 3 miles. Pass a road on the left signposted Charlton Abbots. In a further 600 yards there is a crossroads. This is the starting point.

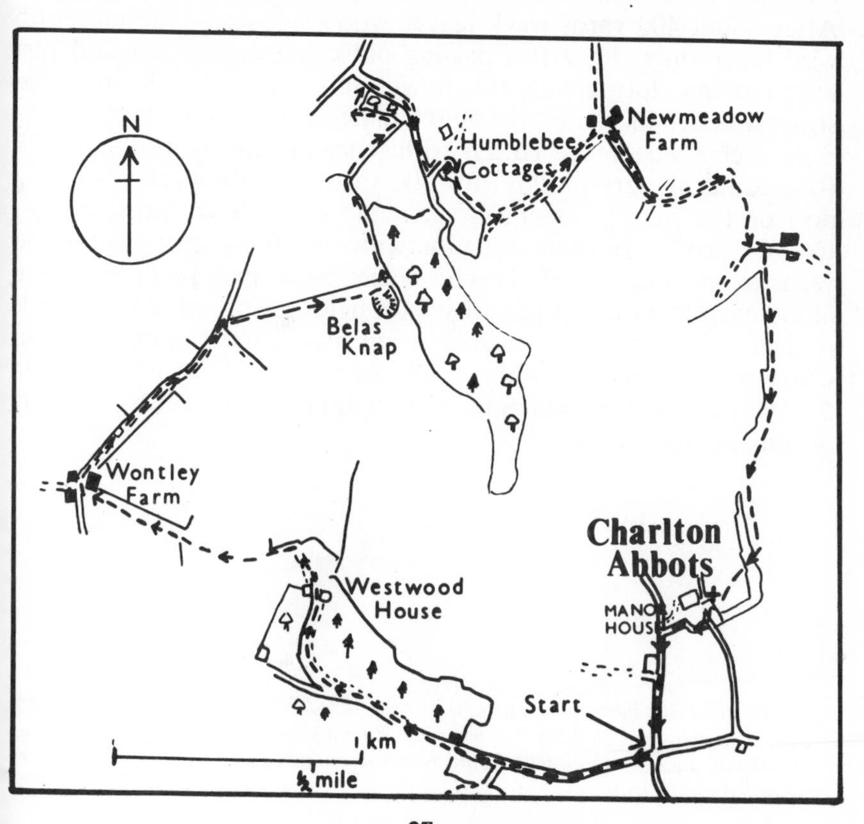

Go down the road on the right, almost due west, for about 1 mile. At a fork bear right to continue along the road passing Westwood House on the right. Continue along a hard track which become a well worn grass track in a valley, bearing left until Wontley Farm (desolate) is reached. Here turn right to join the Cotswold Way. Continue for about ½ mile to a signpost indicating path to Belas Knap.* Walk along grass path with a hedge and wall on the left to Belas Knap and then follow Cotswold Way signs along well walked paths and tracks for about ½ mile until road is reached.

Turn right along road for about 400 yards, turn left along track marked Cotswold Way to Humblebee Cottages 50 yards ahead on right. Here take the right hand track in front of cottages for 300 yards, turn left down and along track to Newmeadow Farm. Turn right through gate (notice saying Bridleway and Footpath Only on gate) and follow track for ¾ mile to Waterhatch. Just after crossing small stream (hidden in undergrowth) and before reaching farm buildings turn right along distinct track with wood on the right. After about 400 yards track leaves wood side and continues with wire fence on right. After passing old oak trees on left and just after last tree, locate wide stile in wire fence, cross and keeping old straggly hedge on right cross field and descend towards stream.

At facing wire fence go left with fence on the right along track (this could be very muddy) for 300 yards – a waymarked fencing post on the right gives encouragement! – to stile in facing hedge. Cross. Carry on in same direction with wire fence on right for 150 yards to waymarked stile in wire fence; cross, pass pool/small lake along narrow path to stile, cross into field. Climb up field towards Charlton Abbots church to stile at left hand corner of churchyard. Carry on up concrete path to road. Turn left and carry straight on for 500 yards to road junction, turn right and in 400 yards join start of walk at cross roads.

* *This stone age barrow was probably constructed between 4000 and 5000 years ago. It is interesting to think that when the Romans came to Britain in 55* BC *it was already an ancient monument. Some details about its construction and history are recorded on the spot.*

RAMBLE 10

Charlton Abbots–Brockhampton near Whitehall Farm

Some good woodland and down walking.
Distance: 6½ miles. Map OS 163 in the 1:50000 series and most of it on the SP 02/12 in the Pathfinder series.
Starting point: Grid reference 032237: crossroads about 700 yards south of Charlton Abbots.

To get to the starting point from Winchcombe continue towards Cheltenham and at the end of the village just past the hospital take the road on the left signposted Brockhampton. Go along the road for about 3 miles, pass road on the left signposted Charlton Abbots and in a further 600 yards there is a crossroads – the starting point.

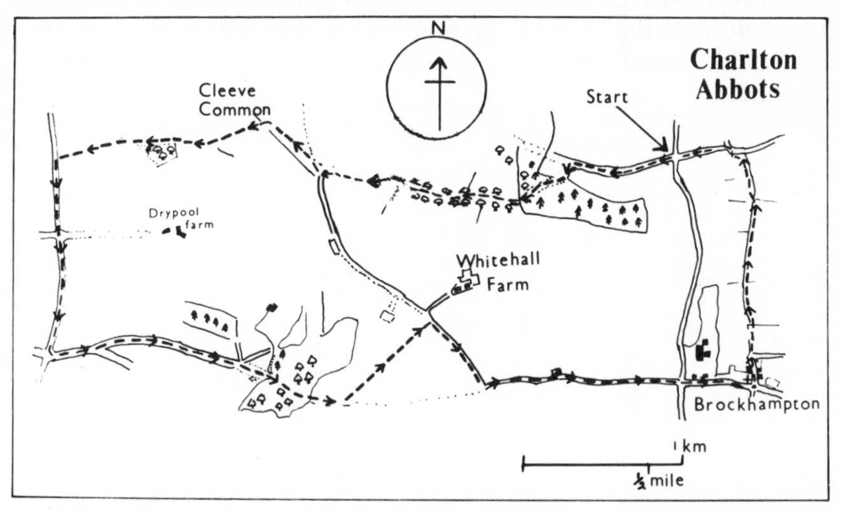

Walk down the road on the right going due west. In 600 yards take the marked bridle way on the left and continue on and up through a wood. At a cross track carry on, the track now becoming a path. On coming out of the trees follow the green track straight ahead. In 200 yards take a left hand fork to arrive at a signpost and the end of Cleeve Common. Here turn right and walk with wall on the left towards power lines ahead. After about 400 yards and about 150 yards before the power lines pass through an opening on the left and go ahead along a definite track passing under the power lines. Continue ahead with a wood on the left, downhill to cross tracks: go straight ahead and up to the road.

Turn left. In $\frac{3}{4}$ mile at a crossroads turn left and in a further 200 yards at a fork bear left. In about $\frac{1}{2}$ mile there is a track on the left signposted Warren Cottages and another marked Woodlands Farm. At this point turn right down a descending track marked Bridle Road to Whitehall. Continue along and up the track through the wood to a metal gate. Pass through with wood on right to the top of the rise to a junction of tracks. Turn left and walk along the dead straight track – with power poles – for about 750 yards to the road.

Turn right. In $\frac{1}{2}$ mile take the road to the left marked Brockhampton: at the crossroads continue ahead into Brockhampton village. At a crossroads by the chapel and tiny village green turn left and pass by the village hall. When the road turns right carry straight on into a field and follow the fence on the left.

Carry on in the same direction over three fields. At the end of the third field pass into the field on the left and walk on with the hedge now on the right to the road. Here turn left: at the fork bear left and in about 400 yards the starting point of the walk will be reached.

RAMBLE 11

Eastleach Turville–Eastleach Martin–Leach Valley–Akeman Street–Eastleach Turville

A walk embracing the beauties of the twin villages with the pleasant upper Leach valley and including a short stretch of Akeman Street, the Roman road linking Cirencester and St Albans.

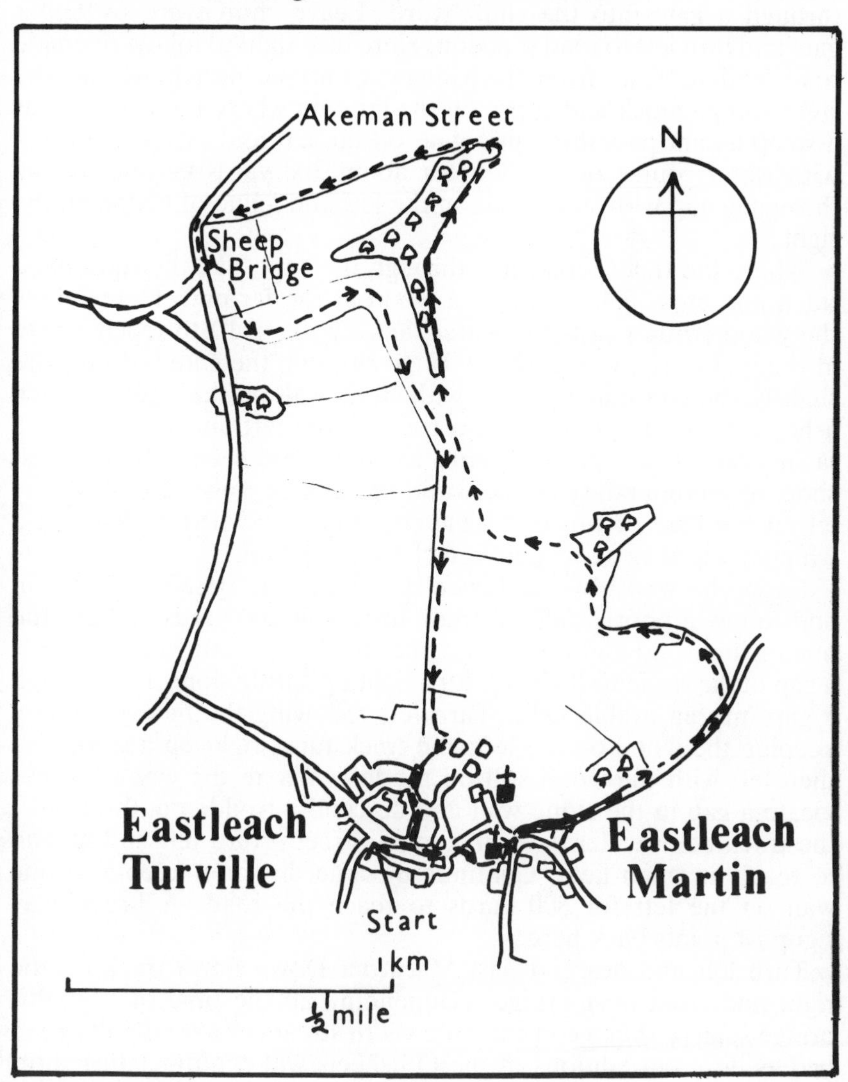

Distance: 4 miles. Maps OS 163 in the 1:50000 series, SP 00/10 and SP 20/30 in the 1:25000 Pathfinder series.
Starting point: Grid reference 198052: Victoria Arms, Eastleach Turville.

Facing the Victoria Arms take the road leading to the right, and when the river is reached, cross by the stone clapper bridge (Keble's Bridge) (see photograph). Turn left along riverside path and pass through a gate into the churchyard. Leave churchyard by upper gate and turn left to road junction. Here turn right to follow riverside road leading away from the village. Continue past house on the right and paddock and copse on the left and where the road begins a steep ascent pass through a gate on the left and follow the track with water course on the left for about 300 yards before passing through a gap with stone wall on the left and a line of hedge on the right.

Where the track forks, just through the gap, take the right hand track and cross field to reach a wood at the far end. Here follow the wood (with a cast-iron water tank by the wall) to reach a gate at the end of the wood. Do NOT go through the gate but descend slightly and continue on grass with stone wall on the right to reach a horse jump. Carry on past a ford on the left and go through a facing gate into a pasture. Aim for the wood seen in front. Just short of the boundary of the wood there is an isolated tree on the left at the base of which is a memorial post to MISTY 1946–51: a whippet whose neck was broken chasing a rabbit.

Enter the wood by the lower (hunting) gate beside the stream and follow a poorly defined track for about 200 yards. Where the line of the wood and the stream veer to the left and where there is a gap in the stone wall ahead, turn right up a little slope and through a gap into an arable field. Turn left following the field boundary keeping the wood on the left: the track turns right up a slope and then left with the wood still on the left. Where the wood finishes locate a gap in the stone wall and descend a trodden path to meet the track below. Here – on Akeman Street – turn left and ascend to reach an open field. Continue in same direction keeping stone wall on the left for 800 yards to reach the road. A bridle way signpost points back here.

Turn left and descend past Macaroni Down Farm track on the right and cross over bridge. (Depending on the time of year this bridge spans either a considerable width stream or a totally dry river bed as different editions of the OS sheets will confirm.) Just short of the Hatherop/Coln St. Aldwyn road pass through a wooden gate on the left into a pasture field. Walk with the stone wall on the right for about 100 yards before veering half-left to pick up a level green track. Carry on on this level track round the valley gradually turning right handed and some 30 yards below the top of the slope.

After about ½ mile and close to the watercourse the track becomes boggy before reaching higher ground and a gate. Pass through and proceed through two further gates to a field and entrance to a farm. Pass through on to the road: turn right into the village and then left at the main road and thence in a few yards to the Victoria Arms and the start of the walk.

(Walk 11)

Keble's Bridge, Eastleach

RAMBLE 12

Eastleach Turville–Southrop–Eastleach Turville

A picturesque walk blending higher ground with good views south and east and, after Southrop, a pleasant riverside walk back to the start.

Distance: 4½ miles. Map OS 163 in the 1:50000 series and SO 20/30 and 00/10 in the Pathfinder 1/25000 series.
Starting point: Grid reference 198052: Victoria Arms, Eastleach Turville.

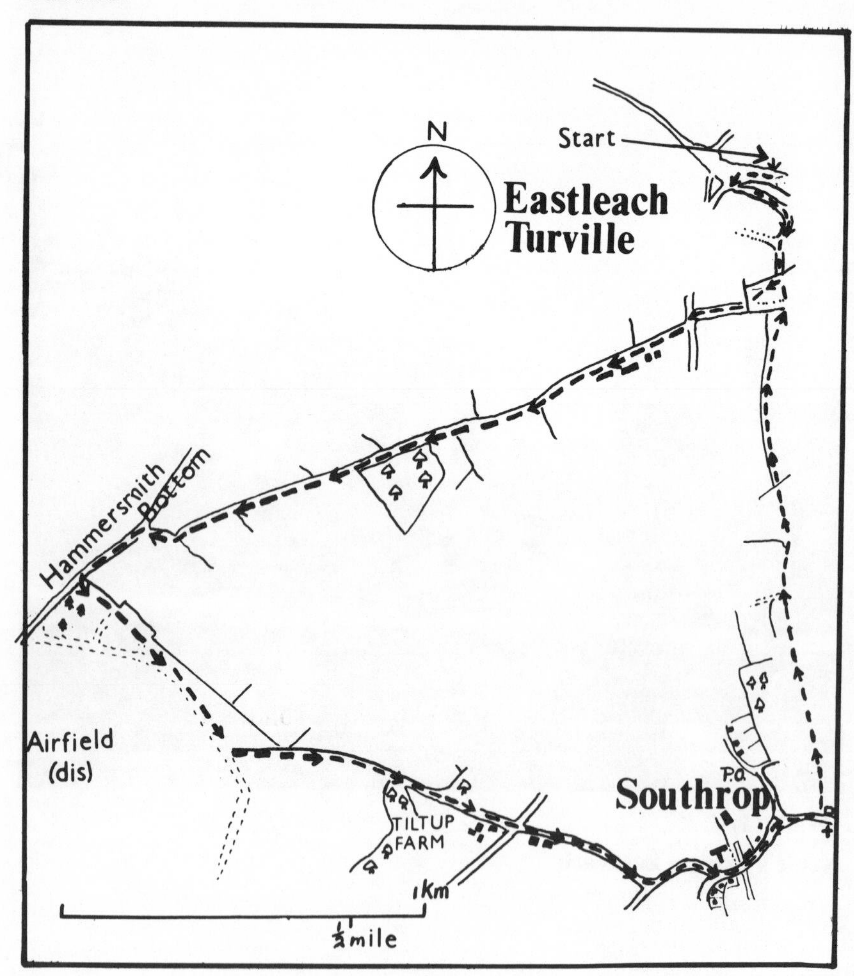

From the Victoria Arms descend to road junction below the facing clock tower. Take the slightly descending road to the left and immediately after passing Verderer's Cottage turn right. Take the first right and then left, just before the pole mounted transformer, to arrive in about 40 yards at a stile. Cross and bear right across the field to a gate at the corner. Through gate on to wide grass path between hedges to next gate on the Eastleach/Southrop road.

Turn left and in 10 yards turn right along a well-defined track past farm buildings on the left and eventually past a wind pump to a plantation. Keeping plantation on the left follow the track for 200 yards at which point the path follows the edge of the field with good views of Lechlade and beyond on the left. The track descends and passes over a plank bridge into two further fields. Bear along the left hand bank of the ditch to meet the gate on to the Fairford/Eastleach road at Hammersmith Bottom.

Turn left up the road. At the brow of the hill turn left through wicket gate. Walk along concrete track for 150 yards and then in the same direction along field boundary with hedge on the left. At facing line of trees turn left on to a track between hedges. Proceed along this track till it meets the Eastleach/Fairford road at Tiltup with farm buildings at the junction. Proceed directly across: pass sports ground on the left and at the T junction turn left to reach Swan Inn. Carry on through Southrop village on the Filkins road.

Southrop possesses a fine Manor house, an attractive mill house and an interesting church with a Norman/Early English – Saxon wall, Norman doorway, trans/Norman font and effigies of John Conway and a lady. Between 1823 and 1825 the church had the curacy of John Keble, the founder of the Oxford Movement, who later became Rector of Eastleach.

At the end of the village just beyond the approach to the church and immediately before the last house on the left, turn left through a gate, close to an attractive weather cock on a stone outbuilding. Keep the river on the right for 200 yards and follow the line of poles through a gap in stone wall. Carry on for 400 yards over two stiles, past a ruined barn and across a track. Coate Farm is on the right. The next gate leads quickly to a wooden bridge and double stile. 200 yards further on a waymarked stile with a jumping barrier alongside is reached.

Attractive views of Coate Mill and the River Leach are seen on the right. Walk on with a wall on the left to the next stile. Cross and in a further 100 yards a stile is reached which was the one encountered at the beginning of the walk. Walk back through the village to the start.

The twin villages of Eastleach Turville and Eastleach Martin are well worthy of investigation. A clapper bridge – Keble's Bridge – joins the two. Eastleach Turville was founded by one of five Norman brothers who supported William I. The founder later bestowed it to Malvern Priory, the deed of gift being in the British Museum. The land was subsequently owned by the Turville family. Its church was at one time served by monks from an abbey near Chipping Norton. Recent repairs have revealed two pillars tight against the wall indicating that the early church was larger. It is a beautiful Early English church with saddleback tower and Norman doorway. Across the clapper bridge in Eastleach Martin is the church of SS Michael and Martin built in the late 11th century. It possesses fine windows, a Perpendicular font, old benches, a sanctus bellcote and scratched mass dials on the outside walls. It has now been taken over by the Redundant Churches Fund. An ancient barn lies across the churchyard.

RAMBLE 13
Cranham Corner, Prinknash Abbey

Distance: $4\frac{1}{2}$ miles. Map OS 162 in the 1:50000 series and sheet SO 81/91 Gloucester in the Pathfinder 1:25000 series.
Starting point: Grid reference 882130: Cranham Corner.

To get to the starting point from Cheltenham take the main A46 road south. Pass the main entrance to Prinknash Abbey and turn left up a road signposted Cranham 1 mile Birdlip 3 miles. At the first junction there is parking for about 3 cars. This is the start of the walk.

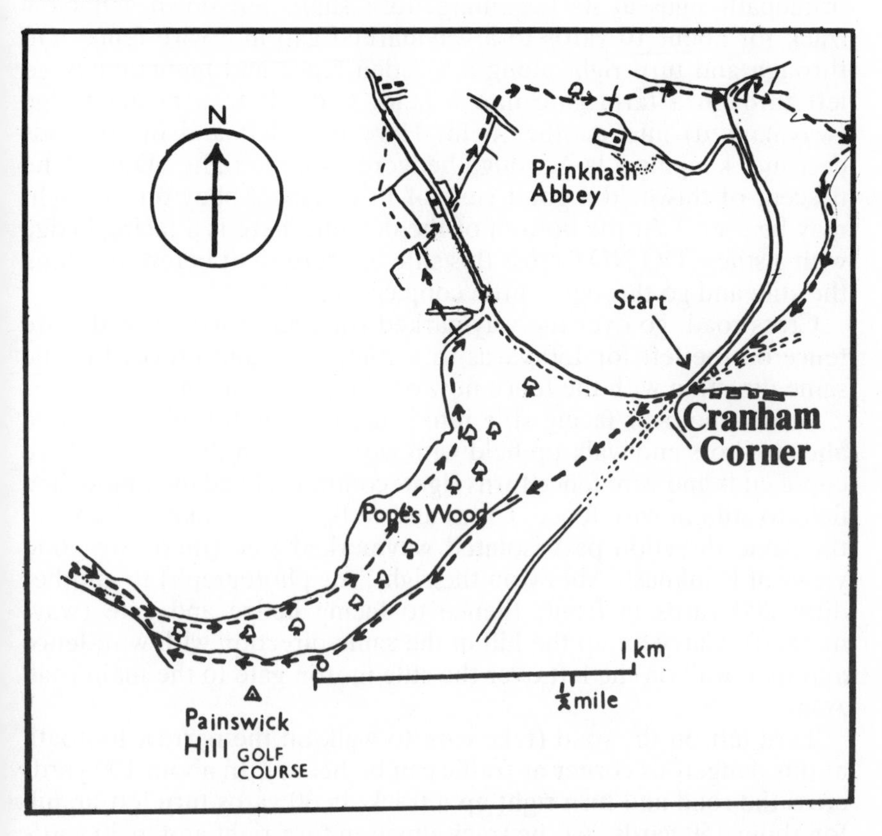

Return now on foot to the main road. Cross road, bear left and in about 10 yards turn right at Cotswold Way signpost into Buckholt Wood; follow the signs, over a minor road for about 600 yards to a tarmac road. Go in the same direction and when the road bends slightly left, at the beginning of the golf course, take the right hand track with a wood immediately on the right. In about 500 yards take a definite path on the right past a concrete water tank and gradually descend on this track to the road. Here turn right and in 300 yards turn very sharply right down a track (and past the front of a large bungalow) into the wood.

At a clear track junction take the left hand fork and following the blue path arrow with a yellow spot, carry on along an excellent path through the wood with extensive views to the west. The path becomes gradually narrower and is often muddy but it is clearly defined. Immediately before a broad clearing with a post bearing 2 bridlepath signs at its beginning, turn sharp left down a narrow track for about 10 yards to a waymarked gap in a wire fence. Go through and turn right along a wooden fence and immediately go left through a farm gate into a field. Cross it to a facing hedge (waymarked) into another field. Here bear left and in 20 yards descend, keeping a large rough hedgerow on the right. (During the descent of this field a good view of Prinknash Abbey on the right may be seen.) At the bottom of the descent there is a facing hedge with a stile – DO NOT cross this stile but turn right before reaching the stile and go through a little coppice to the road.

Cross road, go over the waymarked stile, and carry on with wire fence on the left for 150 yards to a stile; cross and proceed in the same direction with the fence now on the right to a lane.

Cross lane over facing stile into small field with bridge and stile ahead. Cross and walk up field with wire fence on the right. Where copse ends and wire fence turns right, continue ahead over ploughed field to stile in wire fence. Cross and walk up park-like meadow in the same direction past isolated waymarked tree (there are good views of Prinknash Abbey on the right, see photograph) to another ditto 200 yards in front; thence to facing hedge and gate (waymarked). Carry on up the hill in the same direction with wire fence and then wall on the left over the stile in iron gate to the main road A46.

Turn left on the road (take care to walk on the narrow footpath at this dangerous corner as traffic can be heavy). In about 100 yards cross the road and turn right up a track; in 30 yards turn left up hill for about 150 yards. At the track junction turn right and in 30 yards turn left. In a further 250 yards turn sharp right (a barn about 50 yards ahead will be seen) along and up the track in the wood. The path is joined by a wall coming up from the right. Follow it and at a junction, marked with a Cotswold Way sign, go right. Follow Cotswold Way signs gradually descending through the wood to Cranham Corner and the starting point.

(Walk 13)

Prinknash Abbey – the West face

RAMBLE 14
Painswick Hill

Distance: $4\frac{1}{2}$ miles. Map OS 162 in the 1:50000 series, sheet SO 81/91 Gloucester in the Pathfinder 1:25000 series.
Starting point: Grid reference 868118: Painswick Hill car park.

To get to Painswick Hill car park leave Painswick on the A46 NE and, in $1\frac{1}{2}$ miles, take the road on the left signposted Painswick Hill. There is ample provision for car parking off the road.

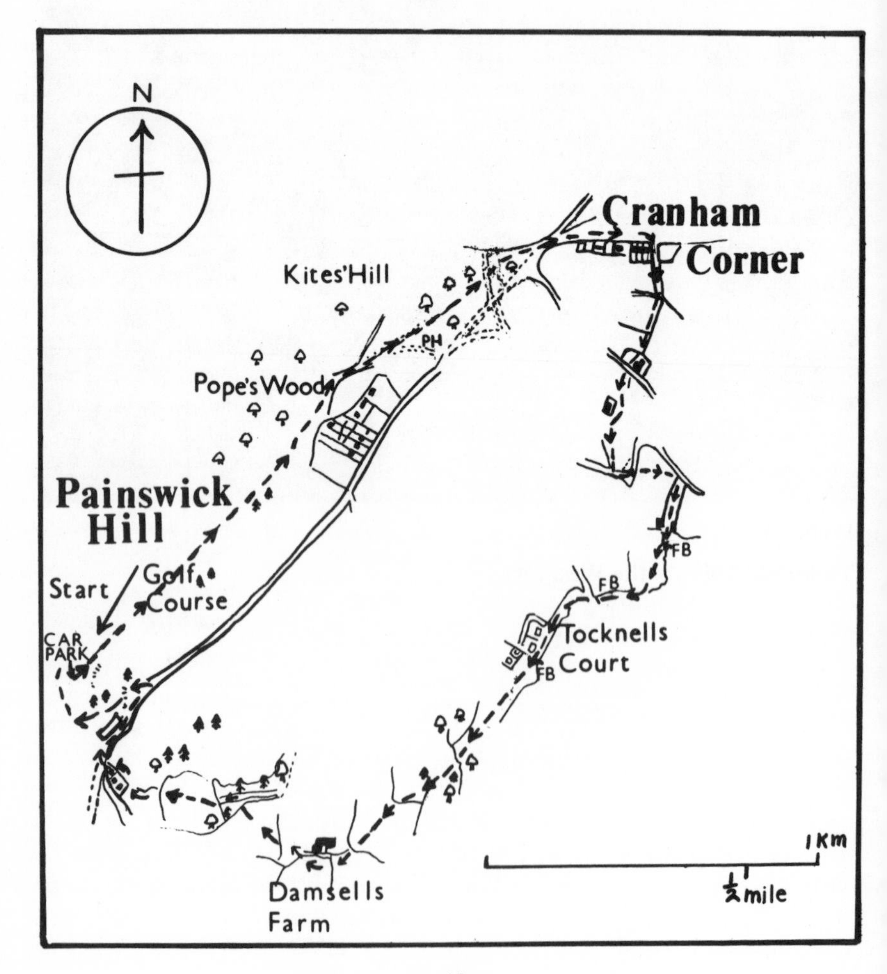

Walk back from the car park to where the road crosses the golf course. Turn left along a well-defined track for $\frac{3}{4}$ mile to where the track joins a hard road. Proceed ahead and, in about 200 yards, where the road turns right, take the track straight ahead marked Buckholt Wood (with a Cotswold Way waymark). Cross a minor road, and in about 150 yards the track emerges into the main A46 road at Cranham Corner. Cross the main road and walk up the Cranham/Birdlip road for 150 yards. Bear right at the road junction, and in 200 yards take the signposted track on the right at a stile between two houses.

Cross the next stile into a field with a fence on the right. In 120 yards, at a gate, go over the stile on the right and immediately BEFORE the gate. The stile is waymarked to indicate a left turn with a hedge on the left and a post-and-rail fence on the right of a narrow path. Two more stiles take the path into a private garden. Cross the lawn to the gate into the road, or use the stile by the gate. (This is a right of way across the garden.) Cross the minor road and follow the farm track which swings sharply to the right down to a house in a hollow. When directly in front of the house, and facing it, turn left and ascend the steep grassy bank, following the line of the overhead power cables, up to the gate into the road.

Turn left on the road and very shortly, it swings sharply to the left. Fifteen yards from this corner go over a stile in the wall on the right and descend the meadow to another stile in the left corner of the field.

Cross this stile and turn right along a good farm road with a stream on the left, to Sutton's Mill. Pass between the buildings to a wicket gate and, in 15 yards, cross the stream on the right. Turn left immediately along a faint track across the field, keeping to the right of the stream for about 200 yards, to cross a waymarked stile close to the stream. In another 50 yards, and before reaching the mill-house, bear right down to a footbridge and stile into a field. Turn left and, in about 100 yards, and after passing Eddells Mill, join the road.

Cross the road into a drive marked Tocknells Court. At a point just beyond the house, and by a small waterfall or weir in the stream on the left, bear left before the fence and cattle grid. Do NOT cross the stream. A stile into the next field continues the path, with the stream about 20 yards to the left, to another house. Pass over the stile and in front of the house go through the farm gate on the right which leads up the track to another gate. Through this gate the path leads to Damsells Farm. A gate and stile by the nearest corner of the garden wall lead to a faint track in front of the house and across to a very large and old tree stump lying on its side. A stile just beyond this leads into the next field. Keep close to the hedge on the right for about 120 yards then through a gate and go diagonally left to a gate with a stile beside it. Continue up the slope to another stile leading into a wood. Carry on in the same direction for about 20 yards to another stile. Cross this and turn left between two wire fences to a gate opening into a rough field.

The path crosses this field to a gate and stile in line with the right-hand side of the two houses on the ridge, about 400 yards ahead. Carry on up the hill and, just short of the houses, turn right along a cart track. Walk up the right hand side of the garden to a concrete stile set in the garden wall. Cross this into the garden and turn right to a gap in the garden wall which opens onto a lane. Turn right up the lane to join the main road. On the main road turn right and in 350 yards turn left up the minor road marked Painswick Beacon. This leads to the car park and the start of the walk.

(Walk 14)

Near Tocknells Court

RAMBLE 15

Bulls Cross, Cockshoot, Blackstable Woods, Downwood North Bank and Trillgate Farm

Some good ridge walking and interesting woods.

Distance: 4 miles. Maps OS 162 and 163 in the 1:50000 series and SO 80/90 Stroud in the Pathfinder 1:25000 series.
Starting point: Grid reference 878088: Bulls Cross.

To get to the starting point from Stroud take the B4070 via Slad for $3\frac{1}{2}$ miles or from Cheltenham take the B4070 via Birdlip for 10 miles.

Go along the B4070 towards Birdlip for about 150 yards. Take the footpath on the left which descends to a cart-track and turn

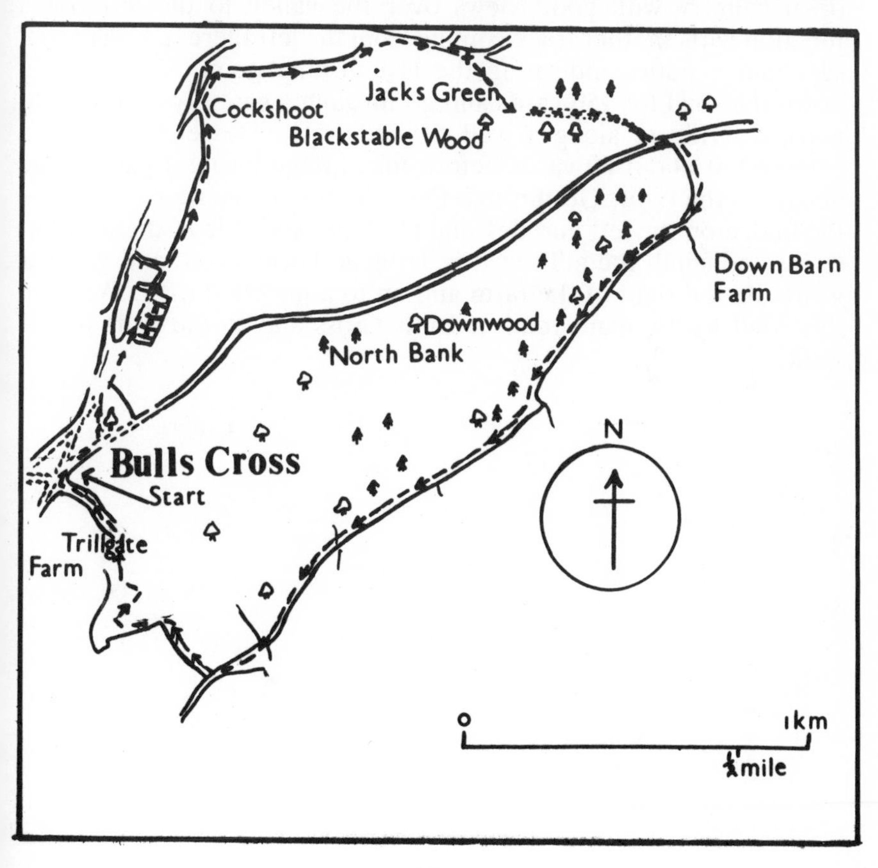

right. This cart-track becomes a woodland track after passing a number of houses to a stile. Cross and continue in same direction to a wood, over another stile to a path in the wood just beyond Cockshoot House. There are splendid views on the left looking towards Painswick. After about 150 yards take the left hand track at a fork: it can become very muddy here. Go past a house and at the cross tracks about 100 yards from road (Jack's Green) take the right hand track up the hill ascending steadily for about $\frac{1}{2}$ mile to a road. There are grand views on the left of Sheepscombe and its cricket field at the top of the hill opposite. At the road turn left for 50 yards before going right down a well-metalled farm road towards Down Barn Farm.

This road swings right and where it goes left then take the right hand track past a junk yard. The track now goes through the wood – Downwood North Bank – for nearly a mile before emerging into open country with good views over the valley to the left. At a junction with another track coming from the left there is a memorial seat and a notice indicating the last turning point. Continue on down the road for 150 yards and go through a gateway on the right marked Trillgate along a well defined track. Descend towards a cottage but about 60 yards before the cottage locate a gate in the hedge on the right. Go through the gate into a pasture field, follow the hedge on the left and descend to a gate and stile at the bottom. Cross and climb the hill towards Trillgate Farm ahead and go over a stile on the right of the farm and on to a metalled road. Walk up this road to the main road at Bulls Cross and to the start of the walk.

RAMBLE 16

Bulls Cross, Elcombe, Steanbridge, Slad

Distance: 4 miles. Map OS 162 in the 1:50000 series and SO 80/90 Stroud in the Pathfinder 1:25000 series.
Starting point: Grid reference 877087: Bulls Cross, 1 mile north of Slad.

From Cheltenham take the B4070 via Birdlip for 10 miles or from Stroud take the B4070 via Slad for 3½ miles.

Leaving Bulls Cross in the direction of Stroud take the track on the right of B4070 going into the woodland, direction SW (see photograph). Pass through a waymarked gate into a Gloucestershire Nature Conservation Trust Nature Reserve. Follow the waymarking along the ascending path through the wood for about ½ mile. Leave the wood over a stile into a field.

With the boundary wall on the right continue ahead to leave the field over a stile. Cross an intersecting track and continue ahead on a farm track for ¼ mile. Just past Worgan's Farm turn sharp left along the outside edge of a wood and descend the field, at the end of which a path makes a slight diversion through the corner of the wood on the left. In about 40 yards leave the definite path and descend into the field on the right. Continue the descent alongside the wood on the left and pass through a gate on to a metalled farm track. In a few yards at a three-way junction take the narrow path on the right to descend to the road B4070.

Turn right down the road and take the first turn left signposted The Vatch and Elcombe. The road rises to a fork. Take the left-hand fork and in a few yards take the road on the left marked Upper Vatch Mill. In 50 yards pass over a waymarked stile on the right into a pasture field. Bear left to the top corner of the field, over a waymarked stile and immediately over another stile to the left of a metal gate. Bear right towards Furness Farm seen ahead. Descend to and pass over a waymarked bridge. Bear right and pass over another waymarked stile into a field, thence to another waymarked stile. Cross into a copse and turn left up a definite track to a waymarked stile and to the approach road to Furness Farm.

Here turn left and follow the minor road between houses to a field gate. Enter and cross the field with the boundary hedge on the right and pass over a waymarked stile into the next field. Continue ahead with the boundary hedge on the right to the corner of the

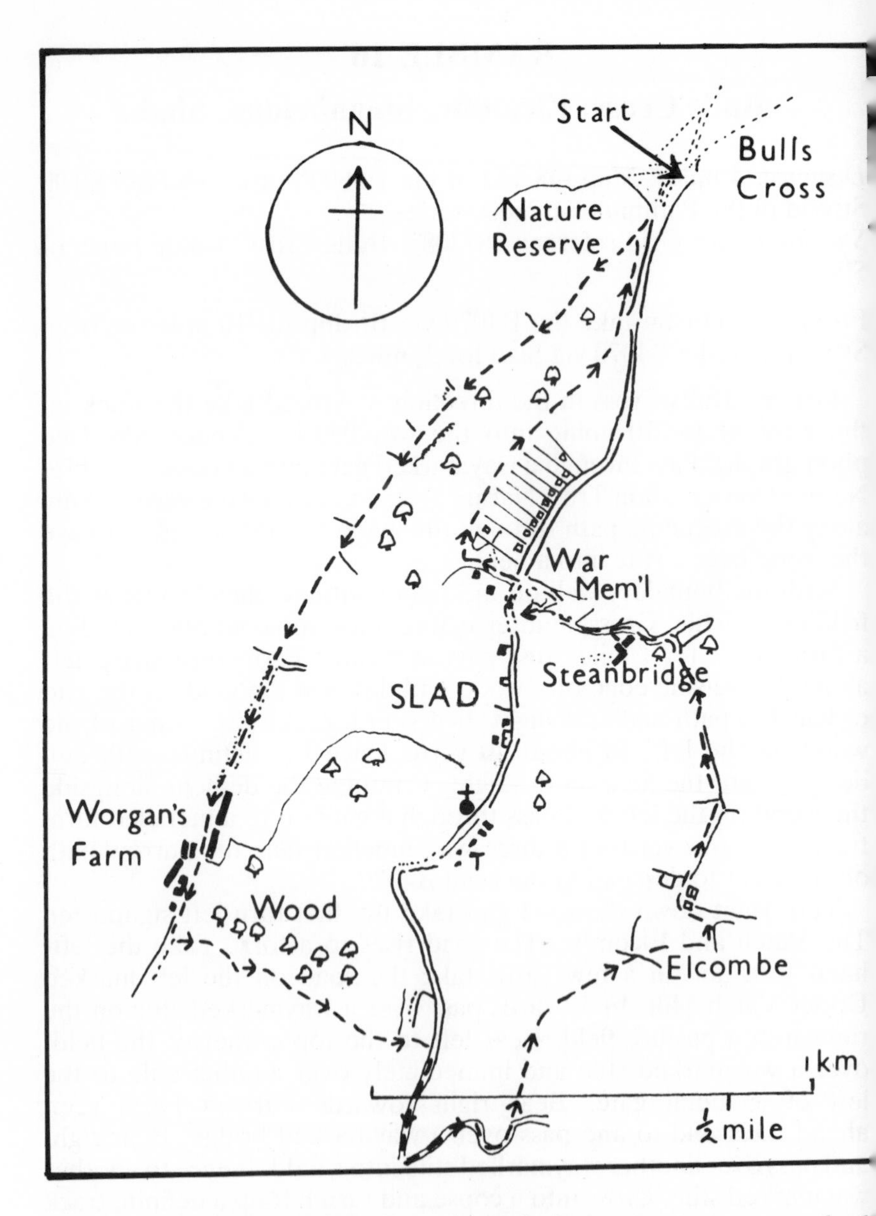

field to a gap in the hedge. Pass through the gap over a waymarked stile into a copse, downhill to a waymarked stile into a field. Cross: bear left to descend the field with the hedge on the left to pass over a bridge with a pond on the right to the road.

Turn left, as a waymark on a pole facing indicates, and ascend past houses to a fork. Go right and walk past Slad War Memorial to the main road B4070. Cross and follow the main track ahead. Where it turns left, opposite a house, go ahead into a wood. At a cross track turn right and follow the main lower track through the wood. Do NOT take any of the tracks on the right which descend to the road but continue ahead to join the main wide track taken at the beginning of the walk. Here turn right to the end and the beginning of the walk.

(Walk 16)

Going south-west from Bulls Cross

RAMBLE 17

Toadsmoor Valley, The Heavens, Nether Lypiatt

This walk is mostly in the Toadsmoor Valley but has also some high level views over Thrupp.

Distance: $5\frac{1}{2}$ miles. Map OS 162 in the 1:50000 series and SO 80/90 Stroud in the Pathfinder 1/25000 series.

Starting point: Grid reference 881055: Round Elm crossroads.

To reach the starting point from Stroud leave by the A419 (Swindon) road. One mile from the town centre fork left (Thrupp Lane). After 200 yards fork left and ascend steeply for a little less than a mile to

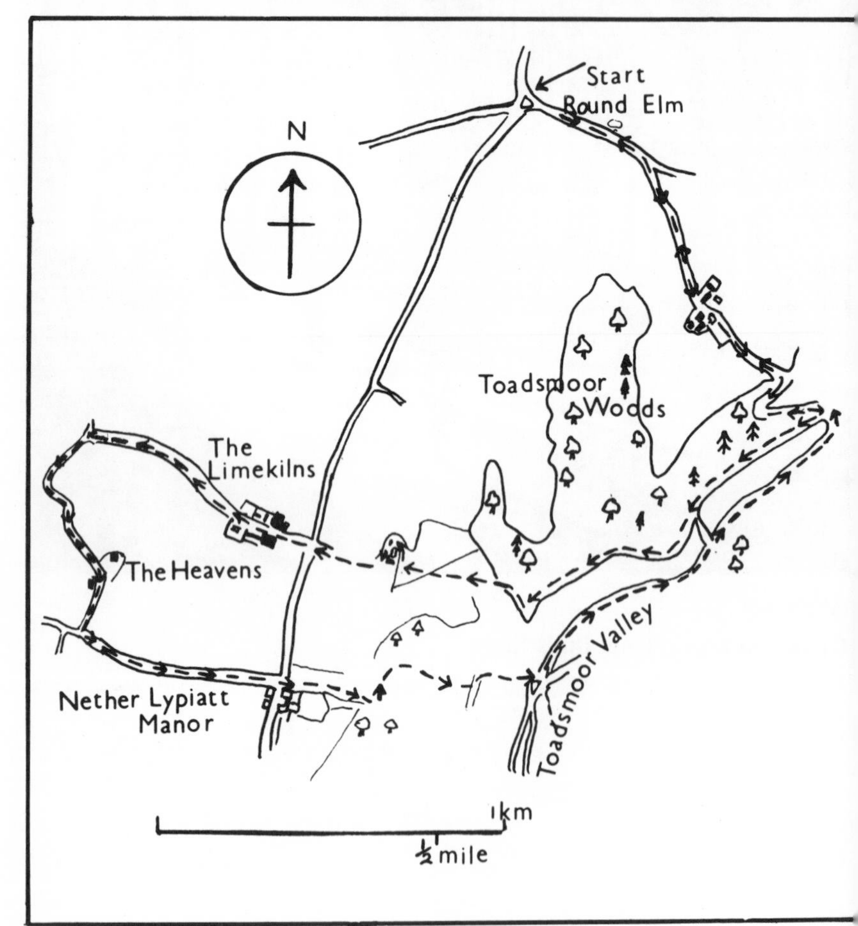

T junction. Here turn left and follow road for a little over 1 mile to Round Elm.

From Round Elm crossroads proceed by road marked Ferris Gate – Home Farm. In just over ½ mile Ferris Court Farm is reached. The way ahead is along a narrow definite path, sometimes very muddy. Descend for about 600 yards.

At T junction at road DO NOT ENTER ROAD but turn sharp right and follow track with a stream on the left for about ⅔ mile. During this ⅔ mile there is the keeper's house on the right hand and a lake with wildfowl on the left. At the end of the lake the main track bears left with houses visible ahead. Take the right hand ascending track for 100 yards reaching waymarked stile on the left.

Cross stile and plank bridge over stream and bearing right ascend for 400 yards to the wood ahead. When the wood takes a sharp left hand turn continue ahead to cross a tiny stream by a plank bridge.

Stile in horse jump ahead is crossed, and waymarked path turns left. Keeping fence on the left-hand side pass through waymarked metal gate to reach wooden fence of house ahead. This is crossed by waymarked wooden gate with a large house on the left.

Follow track to the right then hairpin bend to the left and then through wooden gate behind house (Meadow Cottage). Follow main track to the right to join metalled road after 150 yards. Cross and continue to farm buildings (Limekilns) ahead after 100 yards. Pass farm through gate. Good views ahead to Thrupp in the valley. Follow path directly ahead between open fields for 200 yards. Pass through a metal gate alongside a house (Riflebutts) on right hand side.

Continue ahead along a narrow track with wall on right. At track fork at end of wall bear left to enter wood. Follow well-defined track, descend some 400 yards with wire fence on right-hand side and at track junction turn left ascending. Track bears right skirting edge of wood with wire fence on the left hand side. After 200 yards buildings are reached and in further 100 yards a metalled road at waymarked junction (Snakehole & Bowbridge).

Follow road left uphill for 700 yards to reach T junction. Here turn right for 20 yards and pass through waymarked wooden gate on left-hand side just short of the first barn by Nether Lypiatt Manor – a Willam & Mary period house (see photograph).

Follow fence which is on the right to stone wall and here bear right, aiming for a white gate. Cross stile here, join track and enter wood. At fork 50 yards on take left-hand track aiming for a blue metal gate. Once through, track bends to the right descending. In about 200 yards leave the definite track at a fork and take the minor track on the left along which the light at the edge of the wood can be seen.

Descend to this edge where there is a stile on the right. Do not cross this stile but turn left along a track and descend to a wide metalled track near some cottages. Continue ahead to another metalled track. Pass over and go up the narrow path opposite to the main road. DO NOT ENTER THE ROAD.

Just before the road turn sharp left along an unmetalled track. Track passes through metal gate with cottage on the right; then second metal gate with cottage on the left before joining metalled road at T junction. Turn left to track junction just across bridge and here take the middle of the three paths to ascend.

Track leads to Ferris Court Farm and becomes metalled thereafter. Round Elm is reached after further $\frac{2}{3}$ mile.

(Walk 17)

Nether Lypiatt Manor

RAMBLE 18

Nympsfield, Toney Wood, Uley, Uleybury, Coaley Wood

A walk with pleasant woods and extensive high level views.
Distance: $4\frac{1}{2}$ miles. Map OS 162 in the 1:50000 series and mostly on ST 69/79 in the Pathfinder 1:25000 series.
Starting point: Grid reference 801005: the village of Nympsfield.

To get to Nympsfield from Stroud leave Stroud on the B4066 and in about 5 miles take a road on the left signposted Nympsfield.

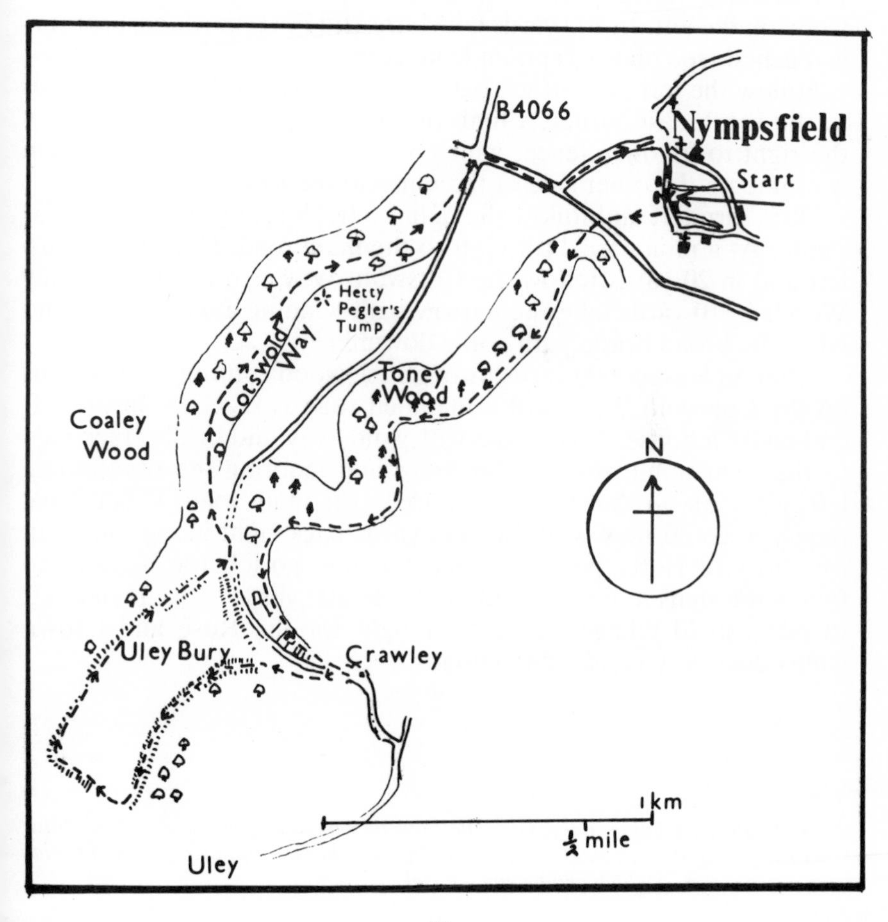

From a point facing the Rose and Crown Inn, Nympsfield, walk left and at the fork go right alongside the houses and in 100 yards turn right down a signposted path between two sheds. Go over two stone stiles on the right of the facing barn to enter a field. Go up the right hand side to a signpost and cross the road to pass over a stone stile and descend into the facing Toney Wood. Now follow the clear path down just inside the south-east edge of the wood. 250 yards after a sharp left bend, where another path intersects, bear left to continue along the edge of the wood and bear left at a T junction to pass some farm buildings. Take the track bearing off left and becoming metalled with the wood on the right, to reach the main road at Crawley.

Here turn sharp right up the main road for 40 yards and follow the bridle path signposted on the left up a narrow track with the wood on the left. In 300 yards Uleybury Hill Fort (north-east corner) is reached (see photograph on front cover).

Follow the left-hand track below the fort and walk the 600 yards to the south-east corner. Climb the definite steep rubble track on the right to follow a fence, which is on the left, for 50 yards, then continue on the other side of the fence to the top of the fort.

Here turn left and follow the definite track round the hill fort for ¾ mile. At a minor road turn left to the main road. Here turn sharp left and in 20 yards follow the Cotswold Way sign through Coaley Wood. In 10 yards take the narrow path winding along the hill and NOT the broad bridle path going downhill.

After a pleasant 600 yards through the wood continue down steps on the Cotswold Way until a metalled road is reached on the left ending by a house. Follow the Cotswold Way and bridle track sign to the right uphill through the trees and ignoring the track going left, carry on up the steep hill track to the main road. If you have time you could now walk the 400 yards back right along the main road to visit Hetty Pegler's Tump.* If not, go left for 50 yards to follow the signs to Nympsfield ½ mile. In 400 yards take the first left to Nympsfield village where turn right for the Rose and Crown which does very good value pub grub.

** Hetty Pegler's Tump, named after the 1694 owners of the field, is a neolithic long barrow dated between 3000 and 1800* BC. *Inside, it has two opposing pairs of burial chambers, two of which can be entered (take a torch).*

RAMBLE 19

Angeston Grange – Cam Long Down

A walk with magnificent views from Cam Long Down.
Distance: 5 miles. Map OS 162 in the 1:50000 series and ST 69/79 in the Pathfinder 1:25000 series.
Starting point: Grid reference 782982. Angeston Grange.

From Stroud take the B4066 to Selsley and Uley. At the crossroads $\frac{1}{2}$ mile past Uley church turn right on to a minor road. In a short distance, at a fork, bear left to Angeston Nursery, indicated by a large notice board at the entrance. The walk starts on the signposted bridleway alongside.

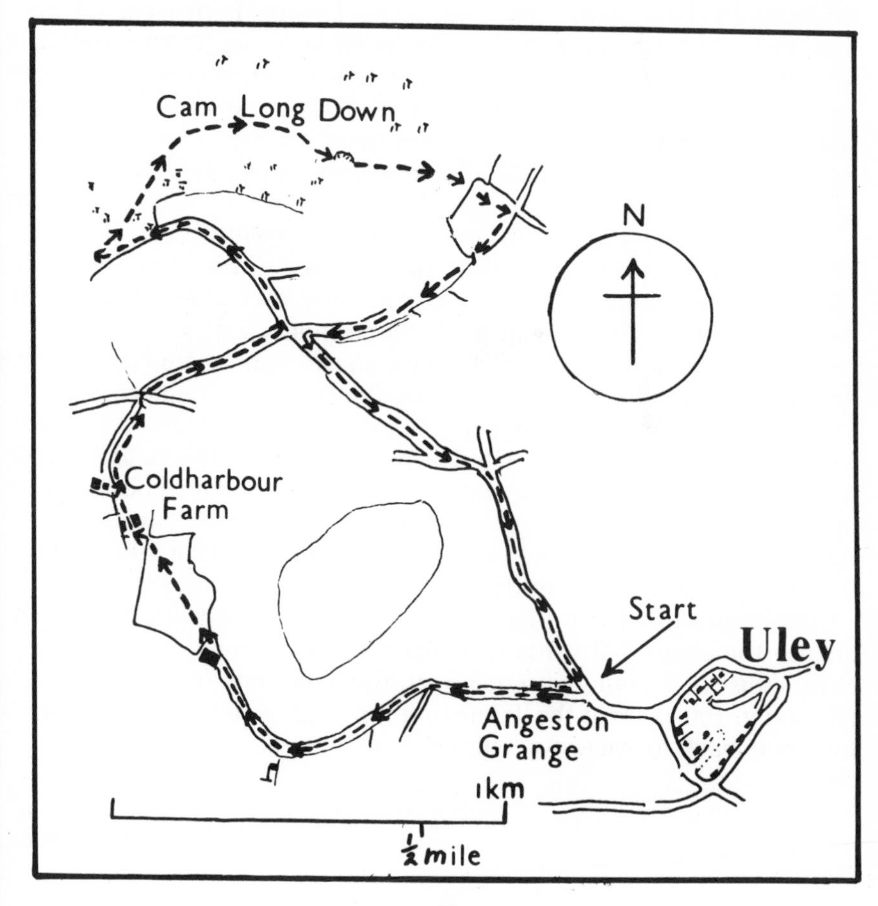

From the road follow the bridleway – a farm track – for $\frac{1}{2}$ mile to end at a facing gate near farm buildings. Pass through the gate into the pasture field; turn left with a hedge on the left to a waymarked wicket gate; go through and turn right up field to Coldharbour Farm ahead. Waymarks indicate the direction through the farm buildings. Shortly after leaving the farm and just before a cattle grid, turn right along a narrow footpath soon to reach a road. Cross and proceed up the track opposite, the metalled drive to Hydefield, as a notice indicates.

At a footbridge follow the road round as it turns left and starts ascending. In a short distance, at a fork with a green track, bear left up the green track (this could be much overgrown) to pass through a facing waymarked gate. Continue ahead as indicated for about 200 yards ascending gradually to a cross tracked depression between Peaked Down and Cam Long Down. Turn right up an ascending path waymarked with Cotswold Way sign to the summit of Cam Long Down (see photograph). Walk eastwards along the ridge still on the Cotswold Way. The views from this height are outstanding and very extensive, prominent among them being the Severn Estuary, the Sugar Loaf near Abergavenny and the distant mountains of Wales.

Continue along the ridge to a waymarked post where the Cotswold Way descends to the right in a south-easterly direction. Follow the waymarks, continually descending, over two stiles, down the headland of a field to a signpost at the boundary with a road. Here leave the Cotswold Way by turning sharp right along the field headland in the direction indicated on the signpost – Dursley 3 km. Pass into the next field – pasture – and continue ahead to follow the boundary fence on the left. Towards the end of this field locate a stile in the fence; cross a sunken ditch to the field opposite via another stile; turn sharp right and with the boundary hedge on the right continue to the end of the field, cross another stile and follow the path ahead to a foot bridge.

Just before this footbridge, turn left up a narrow track between hedges for about 400 yards to reach a metalled road at Hydegate Farm (this track could be much overgrown and muddy). Here turn left and in 100 yards at the T junction turn right and follow the road for $\frac{1}{3}$ mile back to Angeston Nursery.

(Walk 19)
On Cam Long Down

RAMBLE 20

Stancombe Park – Stinchcombe Golf Course

A walk with fine high-level views.
Distance: 5 miles. Maps OS 162 in the 1:50000 series and ST 69/79 in the Pathfinder series 1:25000.
Starting point: Grid reference 736974: the junction of the road to Stancombe Park with B4060. To get to the starting point from North Nibley, go North for 1 mile along the B4060.

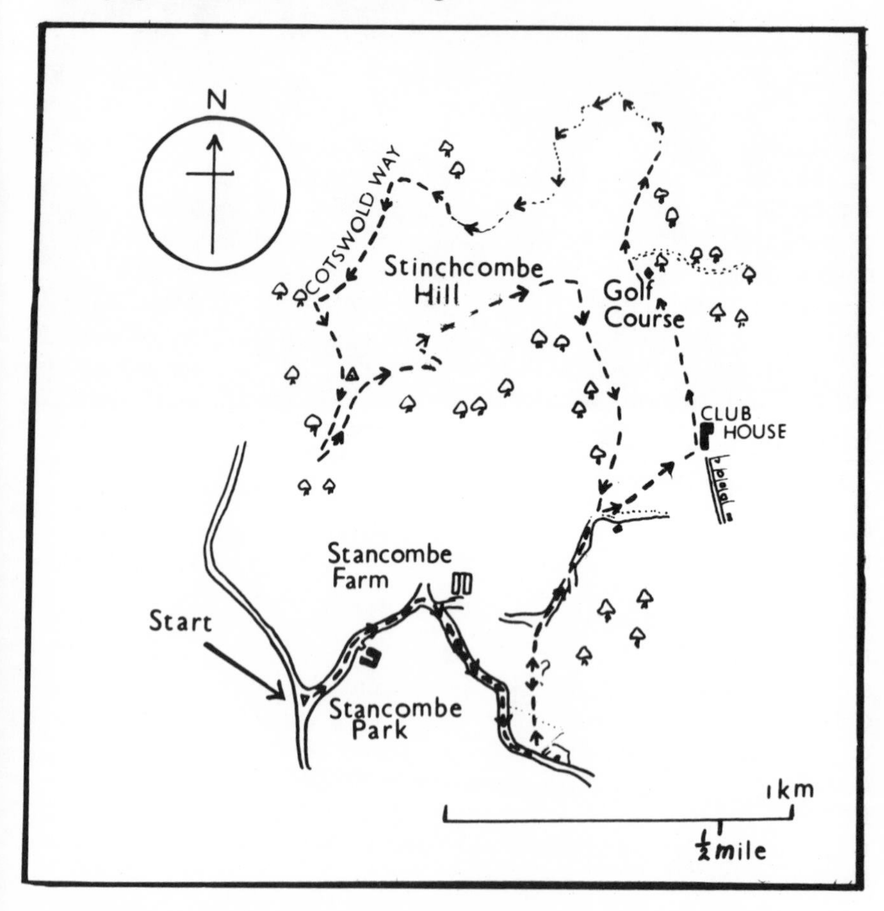

Walk North East along the road past the entrance to Stancombe Park for one mile. After a few hundred yards, at one of the gates to the Park and on the right of the road is an interesting weighbridge with the mechanism set into the wall. Fine views of the house will also be seen from the road. Immediately before the drive to Park Farm House, which is on the right there is a waymarked stile in the left hand hedge; cross and walk up the field to a stile in a wire fence. Cross and turn left, following the fence for 200 yards to another stile which leads into a deep wide ditch or sunken lane with steps leading in and out on to a forest track. Here turn right to walk uphill. In about 100 yards, at a junction of several tracks, avoid the wider path on the left and continue straight ahead. In a further 200 to 300 yards the path turns right at a waymark and close to a well-built boundary wall to a garden. Carry on up the hill to emerge onto Stinchcombe Golf Course.

Walk on in the same direction across the golf course to the Club House. Take the road immediately in front of the Club House, turning left onto the course at the end of the club buildings and aim for the corner of the wood where there is a small group of buildings among the trees. Follow round the edge of the golf course keeping close to the woods on the right-hand side for nearly two miles, and passing a signposted track to Woodfield and a large house. The path becomes more distinct and a waymark appears at this point. Carry on until the path swings sharply to the right and becomes wider, dropping into the trees by the tenth tee. Do not continue downhill but turn left, behind the tee and into a narrower path marked by a warning of the dangers from golf balls. This path still follows the edge of the course, but is slightly below it, to a fine stone-built shelter from which there are fine views over the Severn estuary if the weather is clear. Continue along the path to a topograph and a trig point. A short distance beyond these a large stone seat gives more fine views.

A few yards before the seat, the track doubles sharply back on the left and skirts the top of the bank, affording good views to the south. Continue along this track but, at the point where it broadens out and begins to drop into the valley, turn left at a waymark and continue round the top of the escarpment to the track which completes the circuit of the golf course at the point of emergence from the wood. Re-enter the wood and descend along the track right down to the road. Turn right and in half a mile arrive at the starting point.

RAMBLE 21

Ozleworth: Lasborough Park, Newington Bagpath, Bagpath

Distance: 6 miles. Maps OS 162 in the 1:50000 series and ST 69/79 and ST 89/99 in the Pathfinder series 1:25000.
Starting point: Grid reference 794933: Ozleworth church.

To get to the starting point from Wotton-under-Edge take the B4058. In 3 miles at junction with A4135 turn right on to minor road, signposted Ozleworth. After 1 mile take left-hand fork and in further $\frac{3}{4}$ mile turn left through the entrance of the lodge of a big house, and then past the house itself into the stableyard (see photograph). Therein is set Ozleworth church.

Built about 1130 with early Norman features it is now redundant and is in the care of the Historic Churches Commission.

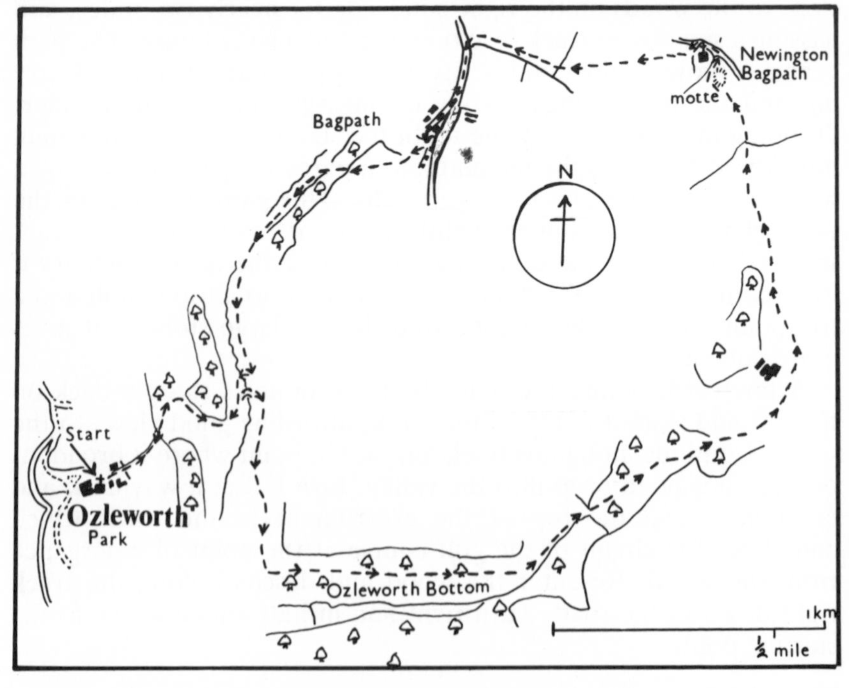

Facing the church turn left to pass through a stone archway and follow a definite track past the farm buildings and across pasture to a strip of woodland. Descend through the wood to open pasture.

Cross to the fence bordering the wood ahead and turn right to walk alongside the fence and follow it round as it turns left. In a short distance the track descends to an old stone bridge over a stream (Marlees Brook). This bridge, known as London Bridge, has become unsafe for use by walkers or equestrians and is no longer in use. Barbed wire is strung across each end of the bridge.

Here bear left and follow the path upstream, NW, for 150 yards to a brick culvert over the stream. Cross, turn right and follow the path downstream past London Bridge and ascend to the wood on the left.

Follow the border of the wood round to the right for about 400 yards to reach a gate. Pass through to enter further woodland the path going south. At an intersecting track bear right for a few yards and then left on to an ascending path which is waymarked. Continue ahead along a well-defined track as it descends and soon turns left on to the sloping side of the wood (direction E).

The descent continues over a water course near a T junction. Here turn right for 10 yards and then left through a disused iron gate on to a winding path still descending. At a lower level marshy land may be seen on the right.

The path bears left (direction NE) to the bottom of the wood where it crosses a stream or water course before ascending. Continue ahead for nearly ¼ mile to leave the wood via a metalled field gate. Follow the path in the same direction across pasture with woodland on the right. Just before passing through a field gate to open pasture, notice a small derelict stone structure just inside the wood on the right. As a point of interest, inside this secluded building is a massive disused water wheel (see photograph).

After passing through the gate already referred to bear left (direction N) making a gradual ascent across the pasture. Away on the left, at the brow of the hill, Lasborough Park Hall can be seen. Continue ahead, pass through another field gate, and pass over the approach road to the hall. Now walk across sloping parkland in a northerly direction with only a gradual ascent. Within ½ mile the church at Newington Bagpath may be seen ahead. Pass through a wicket gate and continue ahead to pass to the left of an ancient mound of earth which is Castle Mound. Bear right to descend to a wicket gate below the church. Pass through on to a road, turn left and ascend the road with the church (desolate and no longer functions) on the immediate left. A few yards past the church turn left through a wide opening on to the headland of a cultivated field. Turn left again and walk back towards the church along the church

(Walk 21)

Disused water-wheel near Lasborough Park

boundary wall on the left. In a few yards, when abeam the church itself, turn sharp right to follow the headland westwards. This U turn, round the church, although unusual, is the right of way. Now proceed along the headland with a wall on the left to the end of the field. Turn right with the boundary hedge on the left and follow the headland round when it turns left, with the field boundary hedge and then a wall on the immediate left.

Follow the headland as it sweeps round to the right to continue through a wide opening, overgrown in summer, into the next field to soon reach the end of the field, adjoining the road.

Pass through a gap, overgrown in summer, in the boundary wall on to the road and turn left. At the fork take the minor road to the right below Bagpath. At the end of the last house pass through a field gate into pasture and turn half right towards a wood. Find, descend to, and pass through a wicket gate into the wood; follow the steep descending path through the wood to emerge at the bottom on to pasture and a stream. Turn left along a definite track beside the stream. Keep stream on the immediate right; follow track for nearly $\frac{1}{2}$ mile southward to reach the brick culvert previously crossed early in the walk.

From here back to Ozleworth church the route becomes a reversal of that taken at the beginning of the walk.

Thus: Cross the culvert, continue downstream to London Bridge, ascend to fence bordering the wood and follow it round as it turns right. Continue to follow it, at the top of the ascent, as it makes a sharp left turn to the wood opposite. Pass through the strip of woodland on a definite track which follow to the farm buildings at Ozleworth church.

(Walk 21)

Ozleworth